FOREWORD: A. L. FANT

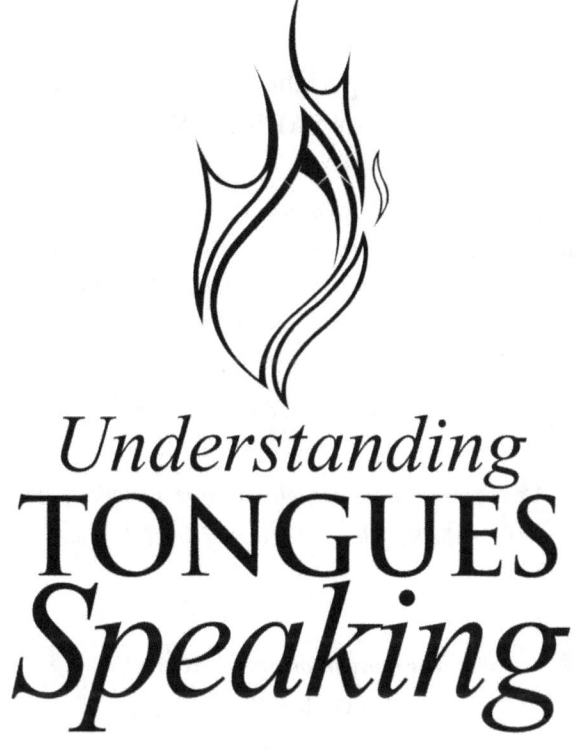

Understanding TONGUES Speaking

...every child of God must speak in tongues!

GODWIN SARFO-ANNAN

UNDERSTANDING TONGUES SPEAKING

Copyright © 2014
GODWIN SARFO-ANNAN

All rights reserved. No part of this publication may be re-produced in any form without prior written permission of the copyright owner except for brief excerpts in magazines books, articles etc.

ISBN: 978-9988-2-0313-9

Unless otherwise stated, all Scripture quotations are from the King James Version of the Holy Bible.

For more information, contact
Prophet Godwin Sarfo Annan
Holy Hill Chapel
P. O. Box TL 2537, Tamale, Ghana
Email: godwinsarfoannan@yahoo.com
Tel: +233 24 059 5785, +233 20 844 7246

Designed & Printed by
MnM Concepts, Accra - Ghana
Tel: +233 244 721 343
Email: mnmconcept@gmail.com

DEDICATION

This book is dedicated to my lovely wife Gifty Sarfo-Annan and Holy Hill Chapel members. Your love is truly pure.

AKNOWLEDGEMENT

I would like to acknowledge the following people for their immense contribution towards making this dream a reality. I THANK THE ALMIGHTY GOD for his inspiration, wisdom and guidance.

Many thanks to Tekoo Celestina and Vivian Amesi for doing the typesetting.

Again, I thank A. L. Fant (Senior Pastor, Sanctuary of Wind & Fire AG, Kanvelli–Tamale); Joseph Kwame Ntim of KNUST, Kumasi; Mary Abena Ntim of UDS and Rev. Ofoe Akunnor of Fountain Gate Chapel, Tamale for doing the proofreading.

FOREWORD

For most people, speaking in tongues is a kind of madness with religious approval. For many others, not only is it ridiculous, it is seen as degrading to their reputation and dignity. The question to ask then is this: "What is speaking in tongues?" and "Why must believers speak in tongues?"

In this propelling and insightful masterpiece, Ps. Godwin takes you on a journey into unraveling the mysterious power of tongue speaking. The depth of the revelations expounded is irresistible; the power of its insights is mind-blowing. You might have read many books on the subject but here is one that will root you even deeper and deeper.

In this book, Ps. Godwin states emphatically: "The Jews speak Hebrew; the Britons speak English while the Arabs speak Arabic. But ***every child of God should and must speak in tongues!*** You are in for great and unforgettable moments with divine truth. Your mind will open to supernatural realities; your spirit man will be lighted up and your understanding of this subject will be transformed.

Join Pastor Godwin on an adventure that will keep you longing for more and more of the supernatural!

A.L. Fant
(Senior Pastor, Sanctuary of
Wind & Fire AG, Kanvelli – Tamale).

CONTENTS

Dedication ...*iii*
Acknowledgement ...*iv*
Foreword ...*v*
Introduction ...*vii*

Chapter One	This is where it Begins	1
Chapter Two	Speaking in Tongues	5
Chapter Three	The Purpose of Tongues	11
Chapter Four	The Origin of Tongues	17
Chapter Five	The Release of Boldness	23
Chapter Six	The Release of Divine Power	37
Chapter Seven	The Release of Divine Wisdom	57
Chapter Eight	The Release of Glory	77
Chapter Nine	The Release of Mysteries	99
Chapter Ten	The Release of Precision and Accuracy	111

INTRODUCTION

This book throws deeper light and chronological insight into the subject of Tongues speaking. It equally reveals the power and potency of tongues speaking.

Many have misinterpreted, some have misunderstood it, others have criticized. However, this book provides a straight forward and deeper understanding hence the title *"Understanding Tongues Speaking"*. It's a must read book and a resource material for churches and believers seeking to walk in truth and in the power of the Holy Spirit.

The disciples of Jesus became strong and powerful after their encounter with tongues speaking revolution. It is your set time for the miraculous.

1

This Is Where It Begins

Christianity is the manifestation of divinity in humanity. It is an intercourse of the supernatural and the natural. Etymologically, Christianity is a derivative of the word "Christ". And Christ means the Anointed One and his anointing. It follows that Christianity is rooted in the anointing. Now the question is this: What does the anointing on the anointed ones do? To put it simply the anointing on Christians destroys yokes. So my dear friend, the yoke is not just broken but DESTROYED. Praise God!

> "... that his burden shall be taken away from off thy shoulder, and his yoke from off thy neck, and the yoke shall be destroyed because of the anointing" **(Isa. 10:27)**.

Sadly, in spite of all these endowments, some believers still walk in fear, lack, poverty and bondage.

The Bible says it was not so from the beginning. You were not recreated in Christ to suffer but to prosper. God never intended for you to fear Satan's kingdom. You should rather tear Satan's kingdom apart. Your life is too full of grace for you to embrace disgrace. Praise God!

Some have spent all their time praying against the devil thereby achieving very little for the kingdom of God on earth. They have lost sight of the finished work of Christ on Golgotha. Satan was paralyzed on the cross for us. That's why we are free from sin and death. The songwriter had a better expression for the same thought:

'He paid the debt He did not owe.
I owed the debt I could not pay.
I needed someone to wash my sins away.
Now I can sing a brand new song – Amazing Grace!
Lord Jesus paid the debt that I could never pay.'

Jesus fought for us and gave us the victory. His victory turned our misery into history. I can no longer be bound. I have no fellowship with oppression. I died to sin and defeat when Jesus died for me on the cross. And when he was raised up in victory, I rose up with him. When he ascended up to heaven, I ascended up with him. Isn't that marvelous? Praise God!

> *"And you, being dead in your sins and the uncircumcision of your flesh, hath he*

*quickened together with him, having forgiven you all trespasses" **(Col. 2:13)**.*

Embedded in the general African mindset is the idea of war. Our forefathers fought for everything that they wanted. With hunting as a secondary occupation, if they wanted meat, they had to fight to kill an animal to be able to eat. To occupy a piece of land, they had to fight the initial occupants to be able to possess it. To them, life meant WAR. Whereas this is true in certain respects, most African believers have carried over an extreme version of this precious African mindset of **Combat and Defense** into Christianity.

This mindset of war is currently influencing many decisions and standards we hold dear. The point here is: Except for some education, most uneducated believers spend ninety percent of their God-given time fighting Satan through prayer. Probably, this might be so in your church as well as mine.

Most of these believers in the end achieve very little. Whereas some believers pray to embrace blessings, promotions and revelations of God's word, others are busy binding and cursing devils. I'm not against prayer and praying saints. I love to pray for long hours, and without prayer I could not have come thus far!

Friend, however, there is a higher dimension and purpose to life in Christ than just boxing witches and kicking devils. I see you getting connected to such a life.

Getting Connected

Every great servant of God has his personal secrets from the Bible. There is something to do to activate what Christ has stored up in us via redemption. You can inherit so much and yet live on so little. There is a class of believers who have learnt to act on biblical information and wisdom. These are those who operate with light and illumination, and such a life always culminates in unending streams of success comparable to none. When you see a man operating at such a high success frequency, you will discover that his success is traceable to two things:

- *Individual callings and faithfulness*
- *Speaking in tongues (1 Cor. 14:18)*

The charismatic move of God brought into our nation and the world a tremendous outpouring of blessings arguably more than any other church movement! A close look at this movement will show that their secret weapon of power has been speaking in tongues.

2

Speaking In Tongues

When Satan lost his authority and position in the heavenly realm, he resorted to lies and deception. He began playing on the emotions of believers and their ignorance to his advantage. The lack of sound Biblical teachings in some of our churches has given Satan a slight edge over the believer, with regard to their position and identity in Christ.

Our generation of believers isn't like those in Berea. (Acts 17:10-12). Most of us do not know who we truly are! The fact that a lie has been operative in church for several years does not make it the truth. Our focus in this book is Speaking in Tongues. And no subject in the Scripture has probably suffered more controversy like this.

Over the years, there have been several negative and false teachings on this all-important and precious subject of speaking in tongues. In fact, some churches do not believe in tongues speaking and see this as evil. To a very large measure, such folks and churches have lost the power of the Holy Ghost in their ministries and lives alike.

What It Is

The words tongue, language and tribe are used interchangeably. These words are used to describe a language spoken by a particular group of people, or for their unique identity.

Revelation 5:9 says;

> *"...And they sung a new song, saying, Thou art worthy to take the book, and to open the seals thereof: for thou wast slain, and hast redeemed us to God by thy blood out of every kindred, and tongue, and people, and nation..."*

Clearly, we see that the word tongue is synonymously used along with each of the following:

- *PEOPLE*
- *TRIBE*
- *NATION*
- *LANGUAGE (Gen. 11:1, 6)*

Before the divisions into many languages on the earth, there was only one language spoken on the earth. By reason of oneness in language, the people in Bible days became strong, mighty, creatively developed and prosperous. They bore responsibilities toward one another and were each other's keeper. They worked together in harmony and in unison; this was based on the fact that they spoke one language.

I must say I greatly admire their zeal. Exploits of these people confirm the fact that "there is strength in unity." Probably, what was wrong with those folks was their motive to reach God by the wrong way. They wanted to reach God by their works instead of by their hearts.

To Speak With Other Tongues

Acts 2:4 says:

> *"...And they were all filled with the Holy Ghost, and began to speak with other tongues, as the Spirit gave them utterance..."*

At the building of the tower of Babel, the language of the people was confounded. Consequently, they became scattered over the face of the earth. At the foundation of the Christian faith, "the gift of various languages was given to the Apostles, that the scattered nations might be **gathered** and united under one shepherd and superintendent of all souls."

As the Spirit gave them utterance, the word seems to imply such utterance as proceeded from immediate inspiration, and included oracular communications.

Before God scattered their dreams, plans and aspirations, God said whatsoever they were determined to do, nothing would stop them for **they spoke one language!** God was not against them, but their motive. The lesson here is that if we firmly unite as believers, our ministries, churches, relationships and families shall grow to become as solid as a rock and as fine as gold.

I have observed that people tend to associate with their own kind as it relates to color and language. Blacks tend to associate with blacks and whites with whites. Nigerians tend to associate with Nigerians and Asantes with Asantes. Our elders coined a better expression for such an observation when they said: "Birds of the same feather flock together."

Why this phenomenon? Language is a strong tool in uniting people than you can imagine. Of course the scripture says *"there is a friend who sticks closer than a brother"* (Prov. 18:24); however, brothers bonded by language will always stick closer.

Proverbs 18:24 says:

> *"A man [that hath] friends must shew himself friendly: and there is a friend [that] sticketh closer than a brother."*

The Place Of Knowledge

Paul instructed his beloved protégé Timothy:

> *"...Study to show thyself approved unto God, a workman that needeth not to be ashamed, rightly dividing the word of truth"*
> *(2 Tim. 2:15).*

Take note of the two vital components of the above instruction:
1. *To study*
2. *Show himself approved*

No child of God is immune from these instructions that Paul gave his spiritual son, Timothy. Jesus, seeing the ignorance of Jerusalem regarding the knowledge of their visitation, wept bitterly.

> *"And shall lay thee even with the ground, and thy children within thee: and they shall not leave in thee one stone upon another: because thou knewest not the time of thy visitation"*
> *(Luke 19:44).*

Nothing hurts God like him watching us live in ignorance of his ways. God has challenged all ministers to acquire knowledge.

> *"For the priest's lips should keep knowledge, and they should seek the law at his mouth: for he is the messenger of the LORD of hosts"* **(Mal. 2:7).**

He says *"my people are destroyed for the lack of knowledge. Because you have rejected knowledge..."* (NKJV) (Hos. 4:6). God's heart is beating right now for his church to know the truth and walk in it (2 Pet. 3:18). The spirit of error is gone out into the world, which the Bible calls the anti-Christ spirit. *"Hereby know we the spirit of truth and the spirit of error"* (1 John 4:6b).

The light of God's word has power and grace to expel any form of darkness we encounter in our quest to comprehend God and his ways.

From the time of John the Baptist until now, man, in our limited minds, has sought to control God and the church. Ironically, the Holy Spirit, who gave birth to the church, is not controlled by man, his creation, or the church.

"For as many as are led by the Spirit of God, they are the sons of God" **(Rom. 8:14).**

God uses the medium of being led by Him as an indicator of one's maturity. Therefore positions and titles should not blind us in our pursuit of Him.

"Jesus Christ is the same yesterday, today and forever" **(Heb. 13:8).**

Let's open our heart, mind and spirit to this old but famous teaching on speaking in tongues, for it's the will of God.

3

The Purpose Of Tongues

Identification

The languages of men serve as a means of identification in order to know who is from where. Likewise, in later parts of this book, *we would notice speaking in tongues as a language designed by God to identify believers to Himself.* This time, it is not His will and intention that believers separate and not become one by language.

This is apparent in the upper room where at the gathering of the 120 believers in prayer, God Himself ushered them into the one and only universal language; the language of his kingdom. This language cannot be understood by the human mind except interpreted by one with a special gift of interpretation of tongues.

Jews speak Hebrew; Britons speak English while Arabs speak Arabic. ***Every child of God should and must speak in tongues.***

When the spirit of God comes upon you, under his influence you can speak many languages you literally wouldn't understand.

Acts 2:4 says:
"...began to speak with other tongues, as the Spirit gave them utterance..."

Acts 2:7 says:
"And they were all amazed and marvelled, saying one to another, Behold, are not all these which speak Galilaeans?"

Acts 2:8 says:
"And how hear we every man in our own tongue, wherein we were born?"

Secret Information

I have a special grace to understand and speak many languages like Twi, Ewe, Dagbani, Hausa, English, Kusal, and Frafra. I cherish the diversities in languages and also appreciate the value of every language. God is a wise God and understands the value of information and secrecy. Believers must not fight against this secret language given to them by God, even if they have no understanding of it. It is best they get books like this one to build their knowledge on the importance and essence of this subject of Speaking in Tongues.

One language Satan fears most is *tongues*. It's one language that keeps him confused and drives him crazy. He simply does not understand any of it. Can you imagine finding yourself in a group of people who continue to speak one particular kind of language you don't understand? What would be your reaction towards those folks? Much more this language: it's divine and from God.

Divine Connection

It's amazing how two believers who have never talked or seen each other could come together by reason of speaking in tongues. Sometimes one can sense a very spiritual Christian by just his appearance.

Tongues speaking is a "mystery", or is mysterious. And by the word mystery, I simply mean something that is hidden and not opened to all. To understand mysteries, there is the need for effective searching, diligence, revelation and time. God is the revealer of divine secrets through human vessels by means of divine inspiration.

> *"But there is a God in heaven that revealeth secrets, and maketh known to the king..."*
> ***(Dan. 2:28).***

No wonder many pastors turn from tough research work. The Longman Contemporary English Dictionary defines *mystery* or *mysterious* as events, behavior or situations that are difficult to explain or understand. I say, therefore, to unravel mystery from the word of God require, divine insight and revelation from above! Revelation is the highway to liberty and prosperity!

One would ask: Is speaking in tongues Scriptural? Some even say speaking in tongues is an act fomented by demons, thereby depicting *speaking in tongues* as evil. What an insult and blasphemy! Others say speaking in tongues ended with the twelve apostles of Jesus Christ. Question: Can we say equally that salvation also ended with the apostles? Emphatic!! No.

This misleading teachings in some churches have led to the no-flow of spiritual ministration and gifts of the Spirit as well as the lack of church growth, and above all the weak unbelieving 'believers' in our churches. Just as Apostle Paul encountered.

> *"He said unto them: Have ye received the Holy Ghost since ye believed? And they said unto him, we have not so much as heard whether there be any Holy Ghost"* **(Acts 19:2).**

The believers denied any knowledge of Holy Ghost baptism. In our generation, ignorance must not be given a place.

THE PURPOSE OF TONGUES

Dear pastor, pope, bishop, cardinal, brothers and sisters in the faith, we must note that revelation is progressive; it's not enough having the word without the Spirit. It's dangerous to run with only the word. The Scriptures are clear on this matter.

"For our gospel came not unto you in word only, but also in power, and in the Holy Ghost…" **(1 Thes. 1:5).**

When a man is limited in the knowledge of the scriptures, he should not draw conclusions by deceiving many souls. Please let's do more searching of the scriptures.

"Knowing this first, no prophecy of the Scripture is of any private interpretation" **(2 Pet. 1:20).**

Peter had divine knowledge about Jesus. In fact Jesus said upon Peter (rock) was He going to build His church. However, we later discovered from the Scripture that Paul, who was the least of the Apostles, moved in mightier revelations and teachings, thereby accomplishing more than Peter, the **Rock**. Rock here means the foundation stone for Jesus' ministry.

Because of this, Paul had the courage and energy to rebuke Peter, his senior apostle, on the doctrine of circumcision. Therefore let's take time to research, consult, ask other pastors or ministers questions pertaining to our teachings, though we sometimes lack the **humility** to do so. God help us admit our weakness and our lack of extensive knowledge of the Scriptures.

God's Grace

For God's strength is made perfect in our weakness when we admit our need for help and assistance. Prophet Isaiah said: *"I'm a man of unclean lips."* Apostle Paul said *"I have a thorn in my flesh"*; Moses said *"Oh God I cannot speak, for my speech is not clear."* Great men trust God for strength.

> *"For this thing I besought the lord thrice, that It might depart from me and he said unto me, my grace is sufficient for thee: for my strength is made perfect in weakness"* ***(2 Cor. 12:8,9)***.

4

The Origin Of Tongues

Man lost his God-given dominion and authority to Satan through the spirit of disobedience in the famous Garden of Eden (Gen 3:1-12). This broke the heart of God, but God had his **DNA**, planted in man that he would not give up on him. He conceived yet plan "B" to draw his creature (man) to his creator (God). The three things on God's mind in doing this were:

- *Fellowship*
- *Accessibility*
- *Dominion*

Man's continued sin, led to the total destruction of the first creation and only to the saving of Noah's family. Even with this measure, man sinned the more. Parents love their kids no matter their wrongdoings. Love has a way of covering a multitude of sin. In many societies, even the mentally retarded have special places built for them, called special homes, special schools, etc. No matter the condition of the child, because that child has your blood running through him and bears your resemblance, you can't but help and love them.

King David wanted his rebellious son Absalom alive although he revolted against his throne. He could not watch his son die in cold blood. How could God have neglected his offsprings for the devil to destroy? Not my God and my father! He will not leave our souls in hell.

> *"Because thou wilt not leave my soul in hell, neither wilt thou suffer thine Holy One to see corruption"* **(Acts 2:27).**

Joel's Prophetic Encounter

God revealed his divine plan to the Prophet Joel as to what would happen in the later days (Joel 2:28-32).

> *"Surely the Lord God will do nothing, but he revealeth his secret unto his servants the prophets. The lion hath roared, who will not fear? The Lord God hath spoken, who can but prophesy"* **(Amos 3:7,8)**

He would do nothing except He first reveals his intentions to his servants the prophets. Note that you're not exempted, because every true child of God is a prophet: go for his revelation and plans today, for real future security is in Him.

God, with these things, tried to raise unto himself a Godly seed: *"...that he might seek a Godly Seed, therefore take heed to your spirit..."* (Mal. 2:15b) who would not lose power and authority, as it was with Adam and Eve, but would manifest greater dimensions of the power and glory of God on earth surpassing that of satan and his fallen cohorts.

Joel reveals the unusual outpouring of God's spirit in a dramatic manner, which took place after the ministry of Jesus Christ on earth.

The only authentic reason for the coming of Christ was to save, to reconnect and to empower the believers (all mankind) back to God in dignity and in glory.

This restoration project of Jesus was dear to the very heart of God. Jesus tells his disciples and believers in general: *"I have restored you to God, only believe in me, I am the only **mediator** between man and God, only believe in my name. If you ask the father anything in my name, what so ever ye desire ye would be granted."*

"Hitherto have ye asked nothing in my name: ask, and ye shall receive, that your joy may be full" ***(John 16:24)***.

For the missionary works of Jesus to continue, a surprise to many, Jesus chooses **ordinary men.**

One would have thought that Jesus would have gone to the **University of Galilee** for a special recruitment in order to get the best undergraduates. Best in **oratical prowess** or students with **supersonic intelligence** that would sway the heart and souls of men to be saved.

However, this man Jesus did the direct opposite of my thinking. Oh, Oh! Man, ***ordinary folks like us,*** because he knew that if people, ordinary as they were, are touched by the power of God, they could do supernatural things for God; see the difference was the power of God touching lives into their destinies. Both Hebrews and Psalms highlighted how helpless man is without God.

> *⁴ "What is man, that thou art mindful of him?*
> *And the son of man, that thou visitest him?*
> *⁵ for thou hast made him a little lower than the angels, an hast crowned him with glory and honour.*
> *⁶ Thou madest him to have dominion over the works of thy hands; thou hast put all things under his feet"* ***(Ps. 8:4-6), (Heb. 2:6-8).***

He chooses the foolish things of this world to confirm the wise, of course, the despised things of our cruel world (1 Cor. 2:26-27). From Genesis to

THE ORIGIN OF TONGUES

Joel, we see the plan set in motion by God Almighty.

Now Jesus was crucified, but in Acts 1:8, we notice that an instruction was given to the selected one hundred and twenty believers (120) in the upper room not to proceed with any evangelistic effort until they were endued with power from on high *(it was a major super-spiritual outpouring).*

Some refer to it as or commonly called it, the **upper room experience** or **Pentecost fire** (Acts 1:8) and (Acts 2:1-6). Any believer with a genuine hunger for the Holy Spirit's experience in his life and ministry can take that glorious power right now in the name of Jesus! Many believers have abandoned their calling in search for other unprofitable works. But Paul admonishes us to fulfill our callings.

"And say to Ar-chip-pus, take heed to the ministry which thou hast received in the lord, that thou fulfill it" ***(Col. 4:17).***

This is our generation and we can't afford to fail God and his people with his power: desire it, go for it, and in fact take it right now in Jesus name. It's **supernatural!**

The word Pentecost in Hebrew means fifty. Fifty in Jewish or the Hebrew calendar is Jubilee which means f-r-e-e-d-o-m from slavery, suppression and oppression. Slaves on Pentecost Day were set free. Servants received double payments as bonuses for work done on Pentecost Day.

The difference is this: whilst the Judaists celebrated Pentecost festivities, the Christian believers separated themselves, one hundred and twenty of them to the upper room, waited on God for the Spirit's outpouring, **until they were filled to the overflow.** Until we go for the supernatural touch from God, the flesh would dominate everything we have and would have.

It's the influence of this supernatural experience which turned ordinary folks into **supermen;** cowards to courageous men and women of God; fearful men into men of faith; unlearned men into men of accuracy and precision; and betrayers of Christ into passionate apostles of Jesus Christ.

Confession

This is the moment for the power of God as shared by many great vessels of God. Apostle Paul said: ***"I thank my God I speak in tongues more than ye all*** being the least of all the apostles".

This was his secret, revelation, vision and inspiration. Speaking in tongues, this it was. Let's dare touch the heart of our generation with the power of God. Please pause reading and start to speak in tongues. May the power of *tongues speaking* come on you right now in the matchless name of Jesus. Amen!!

5

The Release Of Boldness

The dictionary meaning of *boldness* goes like this: "Not afraid of taking risks and making difficult decisions". The bible says, for God has not given us the spirit of fear but of boldness and power.

> *"For God hath not given us the spirit of fear; but of power, and of love, and of a sound mind"* **(2 Tim. 1:7).**

The Bible says fear has torment and torment kills everything on contact May you at no point be another victim; fear is *'False Evidence Appearing Real'*. Man from Adam has feared along in everything he does: fear to marry, fear of the unknown, fear of failure, and fear of disappointment. And these fears have tormented millions around the world and generations untold. This same fear has robbed the potential and destinies of many.

Fear has been an ancient enemy of mankind.

> *"Say, I pray thee, thou art my sister: that it may be well with me for thy sake; and my soul shall live because of thee"* **(Gen. 12:13).**

Fear caused Abraham to lie and deny his beloved wife, Sarah and rather referred to her as his sister. But for God's intervention, his marriage would have been shattered. Job said *"what I fear has come upon me."* What you fear most has a way of getting to you, causing spiritual cancer. Fear is quite cancerous.

Two Types Of Fear

- *Spirit of fear (destruction) 2 Tim. 1:7*
- *Fear of God (wisdom) Prov. 1:7, Prov. 9:10*

The generational curse of lying in Abraham's family nearly caused Abimelech his life and throne. So God commanded us not to be afraid. There are verses of Scripture scattered in the Bible instructing us not to be afraid. In fact, three hundred and sixty-five of these verses of Scripture command us not to succumb to the spirit of fear.

Likewise, God commanded all the prophets of the Bible not to be afraid of the faces of their troops, of which Joshua was the chiefest. Peter loved Jesus so much.

THE RELEASE OF BOLDNESS

Jesus says by a prophetic means that Peter would not stand by him in his upcoming temptation. Peter lamented; **"I would even die with you master."**

Before dawn, Peter had shamefully betrayed Jesus. Now notice this, that this: same Peter was the chiefest of the apostles who graduated from the **University of Jesus, P. O Box 7, Wildernesses.** After that experience, Peter could not trust in himself. The fear of betrayal gripped him.

Peter was the foundation of charismatism. In fact, the Catholic Church calls him the **first pope;** such was the gravity and highness of Peter's position in the church of God. But something went wrong and fear came in. In fear and embarrassment, **Peter went back to fishing, having abandoned the ministry and church duties.**

Probably, you kind of find yourself in Peter's trap all your life, do not despair, I have good news for you. The Scripture has a solution for your kind of problem and mess! Understand this, this was how Peter bowed his head in shame and disgrace. He overcame his fear and rose with an absolute boldness.

> *"And I was with you in weakness, and in fear, and in much trembling". **(1 Cor. 2:3).***

It was supernatural! It transformed Peter's fear into a stronger faith in Christ Jesus. The secret was ***speaking in tongues.*** Speaking in tongues catapults weak men into people whose inner man immediately receives strength for divine assignment. It was rapid, it was fast, it was dramatic; it was real power from God. Please notice that in **Acts 2:4** the Bible says:

"...And they were all filled (diffused throughout their souls) with the Holy Spirit and began to speak in other (different, foreign) languages (tongues), as the Spirit kept giving them clear and loud expression [in each tongue in appropriate words] ..." (AMP)

Suddenly, they were filled with the Holy Ghost and began to speak with other tongues. When a believer receives the Holy Ghost baptism with the evidence of speaking in tongues, the person leaves the position of a benchwarmer and is promoted to a position of active soul winning (Acts 3:3).

Peter demonstrated his newly found boldness. In fact, what actually energizes us to cast out demon is boldness; the power to confront comes directly from speaking in tongues.

Peter and John's boldness was seriously mistaken for pride and arrogance. The truth is, originally we knew who peter was-fearful and sober.

"But Peter and John answered and said unto them, whether it be right in the sight of God to hearken unto ye. For we cannot but speak the things which we have seen and heard" **(Acts 4:19:20).**

THE RELEASE OF BOLDNESS

Peter's boldness from the tongues speaking experience triggered his miracle ministry. Sometimes some folks wonder how he mustered courage to pray publicly for people, commanding miracles to happen.

⁴ "And Peter, fastening his eyes upon him with John, said, look on us

⁵ And he gave heed unto them, expectation to receive something of them.

⁶ Then Peter said, silver and gold have I none: but such as I have give I thee: in the name of Jesus Christ of Nazareth rise up and walk. And he took him by the right hand, and lifted him up and immediately his feet and ankle bones received strength." **(Acts 3:4-6)**

Look on us!

The truth is that this boldness came from speaking in tongues. (Acts 4:16). May the power of speaking in tongues that comes with boldness be your portion in Jesus' name. Satan's plan is to discourage speaking in tongues among the body of Christ, to reduce the onslaught on his kingdom. Have you noticed that churches that speak in tongues achieve greater things in God's kingdom?

Recently, I was ministering in a particular church where tongues speaking, was non-existent. To my surprise, coffees and toffees were served to keep the believer awake for the prophetic program. Why? There was no fire. Why? Their spirits were not kindled with the power of **tongues speaking.** At Bible College I encountered a fellow student who was a Nigerian, who was so ignorant about **speaking in tongues.** He found himself always at an internet café, instead of soul winning.

A couple of months went by and then suddenly, we notice a change in his appearance, language and attitude. He subsequently became the number one soul winner at college. When asked what his secret was, he said, "Brother Godwin I can now speak in tongues I'm no more afraid to tell people about Jesus." Praise God!

See, the difference was tongues speaking. His spirit man was opened up and strengthened through *speaking in tongues. Speaking in tongues* is where *the fire and power is.* Remember Pentecost! When you speak in tongues, you often overcome any spirit of fear; boldness will rise from within you to do mighty exploits.

Peter's boldness was quite outrageous. Brothers and sisters in the Lord, we need supranational boldness to accomplish the will of the Master. Please do organize Holy Ghost Baptism for church members who do not speak in tongues and it will suddenly turn them into church workers.

Paul said "I thank my God I speak in tongues more than all of you" no wonder he was such an **achiever and performer.** Paul's success was equal to none, if one hundred and twenty believers needed this power urgently to run their ministry, may I say we equally need this power! Dear minister do you desire a breakthrough in ministry?

You can't operate in the miraculous if you don't speak in tongues, it's a spiritual reality: True spiritual transformation comes when believers are actively engaged in prayer in the spirit or speaking in tongues. Speaking in tongues initiates you to the realm of the supernatural. "Do you want to be part of history, as used of God in your generation? Then learn to speak in tongues at all times. Praise God!

The Audacity Of Peter

Apostle Peter's boldness increased with such a tremendous impact and power. He virtually became the topic of gossip in the city; he had such power that he commanded the city rulers to pay attention to what he had to say. Notice this time that the perceived fear of Peter had given way for divine boldness through the agency of speaking in tongues

> *"Then Peter was filled with the Holy Spirit and said to them, rulers of the people and elders" (Acts 4:8).*

The power of boldness came from the Holy Spirit *"... not by might, nor by power, but by my spirit, saith the LORD of hosts"* **(Zech. 4:6).**

Peter Out Of Control

Apostle Peter went out of control with the spirit of boldness to the measure and extent that the believers feared him greatly. This same boldness of Peter, the betrayer of Jesus, led him to confront Ananias and Sapphira to their grave.

¹ "But a certain man named Ananias, with Sapphira his wife, sold a possession,

² And kept back part of the price, his wife also being privy to it, and brought a certain part, and laid it at the apostles' feet.

³ But Peter said, Ananias why hath Satan filled thine heart to lie to the Holy Ghost, and to keep back part of the price of the land?

⁴ Whiles it remained, was it was sold, was it not thine own? And after it was sold, was it not in thine own power? Why hast thou conceived this thing in thine heart? Thou hast not lied unto men, but unto God.

⁵ And Ananias hearing these words fell down, and gave up the ghost: and great fear came on all them that heard these things" **(Acts 5:1-5).**

THE RELEASE OF BOLDNESS

Boldness is the spirit that comes from speaking in tongues. Besides, the betrayer of Jesus was more grievous than that of Ananias and Sapphira, because he betrayed the Lord of host, the saviour of the universe.

Paul's Boldness

Men who speak in tongues are men of power and boldness. Remember,

Acts 1:8 *"But you shall receive power (ability, efficiency, and might) when the Holy Spirit has come upon you, and you shall be my witnesses in Jerusalem and all Judea and Samaria and to the ends (the very bounds) of the earth" (AMP).*

Jesus gave an instruction to the disciples not to preach until power had come on them.

The work of God could be intimidating; it explicitly requires boldness to conquer the fear of kings, people and obstacles. Paul stood before King Agrippa to defend himself as a Christian, and out of his oratical ability and divine boldness, he nearly brought Agrippa to salvation as he lamented:

Acts 26:28 *"Then Agrippa said unto Paul, Almost thou persuades me be a Christian and Paul said, I would to God, that not only thou, but also all that hear me this day, were both*

almost, and altogether such as I am, except these bonds" (KJV).

Acts 26:28 *"Then Agrippa said to Paul, You think it a small task to make a Christian of me [just off hand to induce me with little ado and persuasion, at very short notice]."*

Acts 26:29 *"And Paul replied, whether short or long, I would to God that not only you, but also all who are listening to me today, might become such as I am, except for these chains" (AMP).*

Speaking in Tongues is a Heavenly language spoken by God, Angels and born again believers. When you speak in tongues, the mind of God is revealed to our spirit man.

You can access divine instructions. Your purpose and assignment will be revealed to you. The grace to pray for long comes on you. You receive an anointing. I know boldness has impacted my life and has brought me into a place of blessing and plenty. You can't achieve anything for God without boldness. Your very friends and family could be the opposing factor, either under satanic influence or pressure.

Boldness is an important factor in the ministry. Without it you can't do much. What we must understand is that boldness is a spirit.

"In whom we have boldness and access with confidence through faith in him" ***(Eph. 3:12).***

THE RELEASE OF BOLDNESS

It is only stirred through praying in the spirit (speaking in tongues). To preach on a pulpit demands you, to be bold; to even face God in prayer requires boldness. In short, we can't do without boldness.

> *1 John 4:17;* "*Herein is our love made perfect, that we may have boldness in the Day of Judgment: because as he is, so are we in this world...*"

Ministry or the church is not a place for eating and drinking, either is it a social club where members are entertained. The church is a spiritual institution designed by God to strategically wage a spiritual warfare against darkness and overcome.

This war is unfortunately fought on two fronts. For us in Africa, juju, voodoism and casting of open spells, are quite common. Notice, the trick here is **intimidation,** so as not to let the Christian fight back spiritually. Apostle Paul equally suffered that much tribulation in his days but his tribulations and persecutions in the Lord rather strengthened his followers.

> *Phil. 1:13b-14:* "*So much is this a fact that throughout the whole imperial guard and to all the rest [here] my imprisonment has become generally known to be in Christ [that I am a prisoner in His service and for Him].*

> *And [also] most of the brethren have derived fresh confidence in the Lord because of my chains and are much more bold to speak and publish fearlessly the Word of God [acting with more freedom and indifference to the consequences]..."*

To be bold to preach the word in opposition requires a life in the spirit. It also means speaking in tongues. I recently traveled to three West Africa countries to preach the gospel; however, my experience at the Republic of Benin was shocking seeing a whole city in the country dedicated to spirits of voodoo. God have mercy!

The gospel is never preached without opposition. Ghana my home country has ten regions some might call it states elsewhere. Though am from the south, I currently reside in the Islamic stronghold, Tamale. So I know what I'm talking about.

> **Acts 4:31** *"And when they had prayed, the place in which they were assembled was shaken; and they were all filled with the Holy Spirit, and they continued to speak the Word of God with freedom and boldness and courage..."*

From the days of John the Baptist till now, the kingdom of God has suffered violence and the spirit-filled-speaking-in-tongues child of God can take it by force.

THE RELEASE OF BOLDNESS

With what I witnessed in Benin Republic, I encourage believers in this country to be bold, fearless and often must pray in tongues more often like Stephen, who preached the gospel to his peril and martyrdom.

Acts 4:8-13:
⁸ "Then Peter, [because he was] filled with [and controlled by] the Holy Spirit, said to them, Rulers of the people and members of the council (the Sanhedrin),

⁹ If we are being put on trial [here] today and examined concerning a good deed done to benefit a feeble (helpless) cripple, by what means this man has been restored to health,

¹⁰ Let it be known and understood by all of you, and by the whole house of Israel, that in the name and through the power and authority of Jesus Christ of Nazareth, Whom you crucified, [but] Whom God raised from the dead, in Him and by means of Him this man is standing here before you well and sound in body.

¹¹ This [Jesus] is the Stone which was despised and rejected by you, the builders, but which has become the Head of the corner [the Cornerstone].

¹² And there is salvation in and through no one else, for there is no other name under heaven given among men by and in which we must be saved."

¹³ Now when they saw the boldness and unfettered eloquence of Peter and John and perceived that they were unlearned and untrained in the schools [common men with no educational advantages], they marveled; and they recognized that they had been with Jesus..."

Speaking in tongues will release a great miracle of divine boldness into your life and ministry! Praise GOD!

6

The Release Of Divine Power

From chapter one of this book, we talked extensively on the connection between speaking in tongues and boldness. However, our concentration in this chapter would be on divine power and its connection with speaking in tongues.

> "Behold, I give unto you power to tread on serpents and scorpions, and over all the power of the enemy: and nothing shall by any means hurt you..." **Luke 10:19**

> "Notwithstanding in this rejoice not, that the spirits are subject unto you; but rather rejoice, because your names are written in heaven." **Luke 10:20**

Speaking in tongues is fire, hot and supernatural. Before the death of Christ, the disciples were given power from Jesus to carry out this ministry. The church of God is neither a social club nor a football team, but a super, divine and spiritual institution that is called into warfare to save, teach, and instruct.

Therefore to downplay the importance of spiritual or divine power is to open the door for spiritual casualty; the best form of defense is to attack.

The Man Of God Concept

Before anybody is called by God, the element of man ruled dominates his mind and ways, he or she thinks like any of the mixed multitude.

> *"And the children of Israel journeyed from Rameses to Succoth, about six hundred thousand on foot that were men, besides children. And a mixed multitude went up also with them; and flocks, and herds, very many cattle..."* **(Ex.12:37-38)**.

He or she speaks the language of the people of the world (unbelievers). They look for demonic power instead of looking within for the inherent, regenerative power that comes from speaking in tongues.

How Does Power Come?

The very nature of God is power; you can't separate God from his power because He is power.

To think of this would make you go crazy. It's unexplainable and unquestionable. This makes God divine and truly God. However, we can exhibit this divine nature in us.

There are several moves which could lead us to this unusual nature of God, which is power. Bible clearly declares that as many as believed in Him, He gave them the power to become the sons of God, which means to even become the son of God urgently requires power. A diesel generator on its own cannot produce electrical power until it's ignited. Such is the believer; you ignite the power within you by praying in tongues all the time.

John 1:12:

(KJV)"But as many as received him, to them gave his power to become the children of God, even to them that believe on his name"

(AMP)"But to as many as did receive and welcome Him, He gave the authority (power, privilege, right) to become the children of God, that is, to those who believe in (adhere to, trust in, and rely on) His name..."

The verses above imply that we receive power when we receive Jesus as our savior, because there is power in the name of Jesus. If Jesus is in you, then the power is in you too.

This same Jesus said he has equally given us this divine power to do the things he did on earth.

> *"Behold, I give unto you power to tread on serpents and scorpions, and over all the power of the enemy: and nothing shall by any means hurt you"* **(Luke 10:19).**

JESUS paid a high sacrificial price that no one in history has ever done. No wonder God has highly exalted his name among men - above, beneath - that at the mention of the name Jesus (with revelation) every stronghold would come crushing down.

The name of Jesus meant nothing until the cross of Calvary. His obedience to the father brought the elevation of his name, hence power and glory.

> **Phil. 2:9**, *"Wherefore God also hath highly exalted him, and given him a name which is above every name:*
>
> [10] *that at the name of Jesus every knee should bow, of [things] in heaven, and [things] in earth, and [things] under the earth;*
>
> [11] *And [that] every tongue should confess that Jesus Christ [is] Lord, to the glory of God the Father..."*

How Power Is Produced

Our world is a dangerous place to live in. Every true child of God must therefore connect himself to the source of power and should know how power is produced with God. God honors faithfulness; your degree of relationship with him determines the percentage of divine power made available to you.

This means, you would operate in greater power based on your closer relationship with God and the level of God's knowledge you possess. Power comes when you act on the word of God, but sadly enough many have resisted the word of God and do not even study any longer.

The world could be running faster: we hear fast food, fast internet, fast cars and fast connections. Nevertheless, the word of God is our sure foundation. Therefore, go for his word. His word in you will produce a breakthrough and a miracle.

Job said, **"His word is my necessary food."** King David puts it in a better way, ..."*thy word is a lamp onto my feet and light onto my path...*"

Without God's word, you are as harmful as the devil without God's word. Your mind and heart are dangerous weapons to kill anything on contact, including yourself. The only way to be safe is to control your mind and heart through the word of God.

> *"I beseech you therefore, brethren, by the mercies of God, that you present your bodies a living sacrifice, holy, acceptable unto God, which is your reasonable service. And be not conformed to this world: but be transformed by the renewing of your mind, that you may prove what is that good, and acceptable, and perfect, will of God"* **(Rom. 12:1&2).**

Transformation comes when there is renewal of mind through information; thus information is knowledge and lack of knowledge means destruction. So God's word in you is the power.

The Power is seriously produced when you act on God's word through faith.

It's in your belly; it's in your mouth. Produce the power from within and use it in Jesus' name!

How Power Is Activated

There is power in every believer because of the name of Jesus; however, ignorance has resisted the power within the believer. This has led to the no-flow of power. Note: I said ignorance and not Satan! My dear believer, the power of God is not in heaven but within us believers. God isn't going to keep any extra power to Himself for He is power; you need this power to survive any onslaught of the enemy on earth here. Pause here please, and begin to activate the power within you by speaking in tongues right now in Jesus name!

Prayer activates the presence of God. The presence of God is power, so prayer is one of the major ways to activate the power you need for your marriage, your breakthrough, your education, your business, your spirituality, joy, peace, etc.

Confession of Scriptures equally activates the power of God. Confessions deliver the promises of God in the Bible into physical reality. A study in the book of Genesis shows that the things God called into existence came into being because He purposefully confessed them by calling it with the right name. Maybe you are believing God for the fruit of the womb, get a Scripture that talks about fruitfulness, then get in the mood of prayer and refer God to His promise to you, after which **you pray in tongues one hundred percent** within weeks you would get pregnant in Jesus name. You may not know what you are losing out by not confessing the Scriptures. This means your confessions become your possessions. When we talk of prayer-activating power, it's not about just praying but ***praying in tongues that truly activates the power.*** The Bible says God is a spirit.

"God is a spirit: and they that worship him must worship him in spirit and in truth..."
(John 4:24).

If God is a spirit and desires us to fellowship and worship Him in spirit, we can confidently say God desires us to pray to Him in spirit.

Magnetic Aura

Speaking in tongues or praying in the spirit actually activates power. Speaking in tongues catapults us into the very realm of God. When you pray in tongues you speak the language of God and angels, and all these are in the spirit realm. Speaking in tongues opens your spirit man: you mingle yourself with God's spirit. So you receive strength and power to accomplish God's desire, purpose and plans.

"That he would grant you, according to the riches of his glory, to be strengthened with might by his spirit in he inner man..." **(Eph. 3:16).**

When we pray in tongues we make contact with divinity where his spirit and power is infused into our human system. Sometimes this is evident by the goose pimples we receive on our body when we pray. If this happens we receive power, revelations, wisdom and understanding.

The big deal is that the God factor in a man's life translates him from the ordinary to the supernatural as a great and a powerful man of God. The former generation had such men who challenged us with

THE RELEASE OF DIVINE POWER

their faith and made the impossible possible. Their faith in God and speaking in tongues released power, resulting in multiple miracles, healings, tremendous prosperity and had massive souls saved by God's grace.

The power to do these supernatural acts came as a result of speaking in tongues. Men of great faith are men who undoubtedly spoke into the clouds, scattering and earth moving tongues, the likes of Benny Hinn (USA), Smith Wigglesworth (UK), the late Archbishop Benson Idahosa (Nigeria) and in Ghana, our very own the late Prophet Amoako. These folks were great and principalities who controlled their territories by words through speaking in tongues.

I once heard that the Archbishop Benson Idahosa spoke in tongues and there was an instant tremendous release of power, such power was enough to cause devastating damages of an earthquake proportion anywhere in the world, more so Satan's kingdom.

Do you wish to operate in the power and revelational gifts in your ministry? If yes passionately seek the Holy Ghost baptism with supernatural evidence of speaking in tongues. However if you have been an active believer, speak in tongues for longer hours.

With this, you are transporting yourself and ministry from the natural to the supernatural. Great men of God pray in the spirit for longer hours. They spend ninety percent of their prayer time praying in tongues or praying in the spirit.

Recently, the Lord led me to produce a prayer CD which contains seventy five-percent tongues speaking and several copies were sold! A certain lady played my tongues prayer CD at her supermarket and gave a testimony of an unusual sales that day. Praise God!

Bible School And Action Experience

Anagkazo Bible and Ministry Training College was where I obtained a Diploma in Ministry. The college is actually part of the Lighthouse Chapel International Ministry headed by Bishop Dag Heward Mills.

Evangelist Dag is an accomplished man of God in Ghana. His Mission headquarters in Ghana has sent missionaries all over the world, from Jamaica to Australia, Senegal to South Africa and London to the United States of America.

Beloved, the list is endless, with mega church branches all over the world.

What about Bible school experience? Archbishop Duncan William fathers' Bishop Dag Heward Mills in ministry, particularly in Ghana, hence the special relationship that exists between these great men of God.

Archbishop Duncan Williams has visited Lighthouse Chapel on many occasions. All college students loved to hear him preach and speak in tongues. Any time this General spoke in tongues, literally the church building vibrated with such a great tumult of power. You could hang around him but not when he spoke in tongues. His tongues carried such a force and fire than any Russian or American made scud or patriot missile.

Now let's observe his success:

Action Chapel is undoubtedly a citadel of prosperity and prayer in our nation Ghana.

I do not know any man of God who has birthed great sons in ministry like Archbishop Duncan Williams. I believe he birthed several sons home here in Ghana who are succeeding both at home and abroad. These great men of God are successful in their own right and are movers and shakers of the kingdom of God. Their success came from speaking in tongues. Do you want to be successful in your ministry? Then pray in tongues more and more.

Dag Heward Mills meets Idahosa.

I heard Dag Heward Mills narrate how in the final days of Idahosa on earth. Idahosa came to his ministry, laid his hands on him and spoke in tongues. The heat (Anointing) from Idahosa's hand remained on Dag's head for several days. **(We call this transfer of spiritual authority and anointing).** On a recent trip to Nigeria, I visited the church of the late bishop at the Edo state (Benin city), where the late Archbishop Idahosa was buried.

Why are we taking stock and looking into the archives of men of success? Their secret is mainly in their closet: praying and speaking in tongues for hours. I have personally encountered all these men of God and their ministries; believe me, they move in such a high dimension of divine power. They raise the dead cure the crippled, cast out demons and restore sight to the blind. A young nurse who was suffering from demonic attacks and could not sleep at night bought a copy of my prayer CD and played it overnight. Those demons have left her till date.

The power of God's anointing comes through speaking in tongues. No wonder he is an example of success. Keep speaking in tongues; your break-through is on the horizon.

My Little Testimony

Days ago, a sister blessed me with a complex mobile phone. Fifteen minutes later, I lost the phone after I took a ride in the city of Tamale, Ghana. It fell when I bumped into a pothole and I could not see my phone again. I began to speak in tongues profusely; five minutes later I dialed my number and an unsaved man answered and asked me to come for my phone. **What a miracle that came through speaking in tongues!!**

Believers who carefully speak in tongues are men and women of excellence. You can in no terms separate tongues from prayer or vice verse. Your speaking in tongues on daily bases will build your desired success. Therefore start to speak in tongues **now** in Jesus name.

Not speaking in tongues means the lack of power to cast out demons and devils. Apostle Paul was changed by the encounter on the road to Damascus that supernaturally transformed him. What energized his ministry was the fact that he spoke in tongues more than all the apostles.

*"I thank my God, I speak with tongues more than ye all..." **(1 Cor. 14:18)***

Jesus saw the need for power in the life of the believers to accomplish their God-given ministry, therefore they were asked to tarry until this Holy Ghost had filled their heart, hands, heads and bellies.

Act 1:8:
(KJV) "But you shall receive power, after the Holy Spirit has come upon you: and you shall

be witnesses unto me both in Jerusalem, and in all Judea, and in Samaria, and unto the uttermost part of the earth…."

(AMP) "But you shall receive power (ability, efficiency, and might) when the Holy Spirit has come upon you, and you shall be my witnesses in Jerusalem and all Judea and Samaria and to the ends (the very bounds) of the earth…"

(Good News) "But when the Holy Spirit comes upon you, you will be filled with power, and you will be witnesses for me in Jerusalem, in all of Judea and Samaria, and to the ends of the earth…"

Kingdom Mathematics

I believe in the power of the Holy Spirit. I see how the power increases in my life as a prophet from program to program. This is the formula operating in my ministry:

Prayer + Fasting + Holy Ghost Baptism + Holiness + Speaking In Tongues + Grace = Anointing

Apostle Paul was once bitten by a venomous snake; nevertheless, he did not die as a result of venom the of the snake. Why? Because…

THE RELEASE OF DIVINE POWER

"...Behold, I give unto you power to tread on serpents and scorpions, and over all the power of the enemy: and nothing shall by any means hurt you..." **(Luke 10:19).**

At various times in my ministry, demons have cried out loudly for me to leave them alone because the anointing available or present in the meeting was too strong that they could not stand the presence of God in our meetings. I received a phone call from one William. Apparently, his mom had left him at home for church because he was ill. He saw a copy of my prayer CD at home and played it; instantly his room was filled with the presence of God and he got healed.

The Church Experience

I was once invited to minister in a renowned church in the port city of Ghana, Tema. Before the service, I had mixed feeling, of which I simply didn't know what to do. So I began to speak in tongues. I was later called to minster. Something unusual suddenly happened to me: I was literally slain by the power of God within a certain radius. Nobody could come near me or touch me. You know what? I humbly asked the spirit to reduce the anointing so I could stand to minister.

> *"...So that the priests could not stand to minister by reason of the cloud: for the glory of the LORD had filled the house of God..."*
> **(2 Chron. 5:13-14)**

This evidently happened in the Bible: Jesus Christ, the same yesterday, today and forever. Our experiences must measure up with Scripture for authenticity. In the year 2003, at the National Association of charismatic and Christian Churches Conference, I was an eyewitness to the spiritual events that took place. When Rev. Eastwood Anaba began to minister, the power of God came mightily on him to the point where he wept profusely until he was carried away. He could not minister.

God is a spirit, so when you speak in tongues you are charging and activating your spiritual and heavenly DNA, you definitely increase in power and wisdom.

> *"...God is a spirit: and they that worship him must worship him in spirit and in truth..."*
> **(John 4:24).**

God is hot and powerful, therefore you become hot and powerful too. The lack of tongues speaking in the church today has only left us with powerless believers in the body of Christ.

When you feel lonely, speak in tongues.
When you are hurt, speak in tongues.

THE RELEASE OF DIVINE POWER

When you feel powerless, speak in tongues.

When you desire a breakthrough, speak in tongues.

When you don't feel the anointing, recharge yourself by speaking in tongues.

When life doesn't make sense, speak in tongues.

When you do not know what to do, speak in tongues, and listen to your heart or spirit.

If you are threatened by demons or satanist or mallams, speak in tongues to confuse them, because their master does not understand it.

Satan certainly does not know our heavenly language of tongues speaking. I believe after Apostle Paul's encounter with the snake, he only spoke in tongues and shook off the venomous reptile into the fire. God had to anoint Jesus with power and the Holy Ghost into his earthly ministry.

> "...But ye, beloved, building up yourselves on your most holy faith, praying in the Holy Ghost..." **(Jude 20).**

Healing is God's solution to the oppressed and the demon possessed. You either speak a word of healing or lay hands on the sick folks by the power of the Holy Ghost. Beloved, the power comes by speaking in tongues. In fact, without the power of God operating in your life, you are simply a mere man who cannot do any good work for God.

The Holy Ghost is the one who makes pastors, prophets and evangelists, oversees of his flock. Why do we deny his influence and power operating in our life?

> *"... Take heed therefore unto yourselves, and to all the flock, over which the Holy Ghost hath made you overseers, to feed the church of God, which he hath purchased with his own blood..."*
> **Acts 20:28**

One of God's generals, Rev. Eastwood Anaba once said: "Everyone needs certain amount of divine power to run his ministry." How true is this statement.

> *"... and my speech and my preaching were not with enticing words of man's wisdom, but in demonstration of the spirit and of power."*
> *(1 Cor. 2:4).*

Probably, your ministry lights up four bulbs, but I have a **hunger** in my spirit to switch one hundred bulbs on for God and my generation. In the realm of the spirit, there is no competition. Come on brother! Begin to speak more in tongues and catapult yourself, family and ministry in to this realm.

When you operate from the supernatural to the natural, the work becomes much easier than operating from natural to supernatural. We are gods in the flesh (Ps. 82:6). Speaking in tongues will guarantee effective release of your spiritual life for your usage and to the benefit of the kingdom.

"I have said, ye [are] gods; and all of you [are] children of the most High." **Ps. 82:6**

God speaks in several ways, but one of the major ways is through tongues speaking in prayer. Speaking in tongues rids your mind of filth for divine clarity. For generations, Satan has sought for deceptions regarding the power ministry and has labeled every minister who moves in power as fake, money-minded or power-drunk. But we are not ignorant of his devices. We will resist him with the power of the Holy Ghost through speaking in tongues (James 4:7).

The power ministry and tongues speaking are interconnected, simply inseparable. Where there is no spirit baptism, there is no demonstration of power of the Holy Ghost.

You would be greatly amazed if we began to speak in tongues daily, constantly monitoring your progress. Jesus Christ, the author and finisher of our faith, desires that we speak in tongues to release the divine power in us and with us. Receive there lease of divine power in your ministry, marriage and family today. Stay connected to the ministry of speaking in tongues.

> *"...For the kingdom of God is not in word, but in power..." **(1 Cor. 4: 20).***

In conclusion, John the beloved was also known as John the divine because he understood and operated in love and tongues speaking. Bible history recalls that the Romans fried him in hot oil. The more they fried him, the more he lived.

Finally, he disappeared to the island of Patmos, where he received the book of Revelation in writing. He was such a founder in his generation. Oh God help us to be founders in our generation I pray! 1 Cor. 6:19, If our body is the temple of the Holy Ghost, then we carry power for our generation.

Years went by with me yeaning to experience God's power when, suddenly, at a meeting in Accra the man of God singled me out to come. Upon getting to him, I was heavily slain by the anointing on him. I will never forget this experience.

7

The Release Of Divine Wisdom

Another name of Jesus Christ is wisdom; therefore the vehicle and passengers of Christianity are all called wisdom. In fact the Bible says wisdom from above is the principal thing. Note: "The principal thing" meaning the main subject of attention. As faith acts on God's word, wisdom is inevitable in building our spiritual foundation.

The Bible says there are two types of wisdom:

- **Human wisdom**(sensual wisdom) sensual – 'acquired knowledge'.
- **Godly wisdom** (James, 1 Cor. 1:26).

Human wisdom exalts man. Paul had this to say:

> "That your faith should not stand in the wisdom of men, but in the power of God".
> **1 Cor. 2:5**

Without God in your earthly wisdom it is a deadly and destructive thing. I'm not against it because I gained earthly wisdom from my environment and teachers at school. Thus Human wisdom is relevant but not in comparison to divine wisdom. Contemporary earthly wisdom denies the existence of God.

Divine Wisdom

Wisdom is a spirit of excellence from God to man that causes him to excel and operate from the dimension of God. God's foolishness is wiser than the wisdom of man in every sense, the Bible says.

> *"Because the foolishness of God is wiser than men; and the weakness of God is stronger than men..."* **1 Cor. 1:25**

What has speaking in tongues got to do with wisdom? Dear Reverend, the connection is so obvious you would miss out on this. The upper room experience in the book of Acts is the bed rock for divine wisdom for believers after the resurrection of Jesus Christ.

Apostle Paul spoke much about wisdom to the Corinthian church while in prison. Our Christian warfare today requires intensive knowledge of God's word, wisdom and power to win every winnable battle in our faith and life.

THE RELEASE OF DIVINE WISDOM

Paul encountered Agrippa, the king who supposedly had the power to decide Paul's faith, in judgment. Paul planed and longed for a lifetime opportunity to preach the gospel to the authority.

The narration of history turned into a preaching, which saved others and nearly saved Agrippa. This was pure wisdom from above. Paul's constant speaking in tongues triggered an unusual success with wisdom.

"...Therefore, brethren, be eager to prophesy. And forbid not to speak with tongues..."
(1 Cor. 14:39).

God operates by wisdom. Heaven operates through wisdom. As we speak more in tongues, we tap into divine wisdom from above. Speaking in tongues releases the mind of God. The Bible says when God speaks the wise listen.

Question : How do you intend to hear the voice of God?

I recently listened to a great man of God in our generation talk about his miracle ministry and the successes achieved. He attributed all to speaking in tongues and taking spirit-led decisions.

You see these spirit-led decisions are what we call wisdom. Taking steps based on revealed information from the throne room of grace. This was Paul's prayer for the Colossian church (Col. 1:9, 10).

We cannot walk worthy of the lord without wisdom.

> " ...For this cause we also, since the day we heard [it], do not cease to pray for you, and to desire that ye might be filled with the knowledge of his will in all wisdom and spiritual understanding;
>
> "That ye might walk worthy of the Lord unto all pleasing, being fruitful in every good work, and increasing in the knowledge of God..." **Col 1:9-10**

Wisdom is the principal ingredient for life. Wisdom is not common to the ordinal man; neither does wisdom come with age. That means that agedness is not always wisdom.

Life in itself is the center of the valley of decision. Everyday of our life, we have no option but to make a decision.

Life without decision making is disaster making. My desire is to highlight and connect the transformation power of tongues speaking with wisdom from above. Wisdom is a spirit, more so a spirit of excellence from God to man that causes him to supernaturally excel and also operate from the dimension of God.

The Bible says the wisdom from God is a million times better than any wisdom from his created beings. Think of this; it is basically incomparable to none. I have seen many believers who are languishing and wallowing in poverty and this always lead me to tears. The Bible says it was not so from the beginning.

The ability to create wealth to overcome poverty is purely wisdom. How can we take advantage of what has been made available to us? After praying in tongues for long, please listen to your heart and the Holy Spirit will drop creative ideas, some witty invention, and some financial wisdom to elevate you from poverty to plenty.

Levels Of Wisdom

In every institution we have classes. In every social setting, we have levels. So to talk of levels of wisdom is greatly accurate in this regard.

Level One

WISDOM AND THE WORD OF GOD

The Scriptures have the power to make us wise when studied. Various Bible characters boosted of their wisdom and achievement in relation to the word of God.

What we must understand is this: the subject wisdom has confused many over the years, but the truth of the matter is that when the subject of wisdom is taught with patience and diligence it can comprehended with ease:

An elderly counsel is wisdom.
Inspiration from God is wisdom.
Revelation from God is wisdom.
Institutional counseling and guidance is wisdom.
Advice from a matured and experienced person is wisdom.
God-sent angelic visitation is wisdom.
A pastor's counsel is wisdom.
Godly parental counsel is wisdom.

There are such people planted around you who have excelled in the area where you are involved and still trying to find your feet. It is wisdom to line up behind them and grab what they have to offer.

All these, are or could be, God-sent wisdom to you. We should be careful and not miss out on any of these. God could also send wisdom through tongues speaking.

King Solomon was the greatest king in his generation who exhibited an accumulation of wealth and wisdom. What opened Solomon up for wisdom was that he requested wisdom from God, and he was granted.

Our born-again generation is better than that of Solomon, so ask God for wisdom.

THE RELEASE OF DIVINE WISDOM

1 Kings 4:34, "And there came of all people to hear the Wisdom of Solomon, from all kings of the earth, which had heard of his wisdom..."

You might have the ideas, vision, purpose and plans, but without wisdom it will not amount to anything. The Bible declares: *"Wisdom builds a house and not money."* Have you thought of this my dear friend, that, money does not build but wisdom? Amazingly, many are deceived into thinking money is everything, but it is not so with God.

Give attention to your Scriptures, study and pray for wisdom from God to succeed in all your undertakings, for this is one for the surest ways to stay on top. I believe that in our dispensation, one of the cardinal principles we must apply is the principle of the **"go get wisdom attitude".**

Wisdom is not gotten on a silver platter; in fact, the book of Proverbs says *"she's a precious ornament more than gold and silver."* Do you know how gold and silver are extracted from the underground?

Three things are required:

Your time: Time is vital in our quest for divine wisdom. Many give up easily and such folks do not receive anything from God Almighty. It is said that one's love is not in words but in the investment of quality time; so test our maturity and love for him by the quality of time we spend in his presence. The mark of Satan is that he moves from one place to the other; he has no fixed address and I know you are not satan so spend time with God.

Diligence: Being careful and always constant will usher you into a different realm of wisdom. Diligence in what? In the presence of God and in the Scriptures. Initially, your accumulation of wisdom might not be known to you; however, it will not go unnoticed by friends, colleagues, and other people.

Hard work: As I stated earlier, gold and silver can't be compared to wisdom or the price of wisdom – it is more than gold and silver. So if it is difficult to extract gold and silver that means you need extraordinary strength to lay hands on wisdom. So go for wisdom the hard way.

Level Two

SPEAKING IN TONGUES
AND THE RELEASE OF WISDOM

In this book, our attention has mainly been on speaking in tongues. Let's take time to examine the relationship that exists between speaking in tongues and wisdom. Men who were stupid or cowards in the Scriptures became men of wisdom overnight through the agency of speaking in tongues. The wisdom of speaking in tongues comes directly to our spirit through the means of divine inspiration.

THE RELEASE OF DIVINE WISDOM

Apostle Paul was noted for the unusual wisdom he demonstrated through the epistles he wrote to the various churches he planted. His understanding into the matters of his days were as a result of his divine wisdom impacted into his spirit through speaking in tongues, which made him outstanding.

Wisdom as a spirit is therefore impacted or caught. Through the medium of another vessel of wisdom, you can equally receive wisdom as you read this book.

My father and Bishop in the ministry, is Bishop Charles Agyin Asare. A man who started in a small way in the city of Tamale has now become a worldwide phenomenon impacting lives with the Gospel of Jesus Christ.

Regularly, I get invitations to the Ghana Prison High Command to preach to the officers. By God's grace we also conduct ourselves wisely to win their respect and confidence. It takes wisdom to handle yourself among the security forces.

From the beginning, he was limited in resources, finances and personnel, but one thing I do know about him is the uncommon wisdom he possesses. This great man of God is gifted with divine wisdom and **I do know he is a man of prayer who prays for almost seven hours in tongues non-stop. No wonder he is regularly called for national prayer assignments.**

It takes wisdom to meet and relate to people with different cultures and nationality. My Bishop has it all with wisdom. What am trying to depict here is that when you pray and speak in tongues for a long time, the spirit of wisdom is infused into your spirit man, who makes your decisions, thinking and doing great to the amazement of many and to the glory of God.

There is uncommon wisdom that comes with speaking in tongues; go for this wisdom by speaking in tongues anytime you pray. Your spirit taps into the spirit of wisdom from the throne of God when you pray in tongues.

Wisdom is application of knowledge intelligently. Our God is the most super-intelligent being ever. When we apply his instruction, what we receive through speaking in tongues is wisdom. Wisdom is the principal thing; therefore in all your getting get understanding.

Jesus is the wisdom and power of God .

> *"But unto them which are called, both Jews and Greeks, Christ the power of God, and the wisdom of God..." **(1 Cor. 1:24)***

Wisdom is not merely the accumulation of knowledge built but also the assimilation of the word. Wisdom is the major preserver of life, not money. A foolish man will perish with much financial prosperity (Prov. 1:32). King David remarks in Psalm 90:12 that teach us to number our days so we may apply our hearts to wisdom.

Ps. 90:12, *"...so teach [us] to number our days, that we may apply [our] hearts unto wisdom..."*

Wisdom To Solve Problems

Paul, with the Corinthian church, had serious problems to deal with. It was that the young Apollos began to excel like Paul, and then arose in comparison of Paul's work and that of Apollos. But Paul was smart and quick to respond that he planted and Apollos watered and God gave the increase. A novice would have projected himself in that matter to worsen the situation, but Paul was wiser than that.

1 Cor. 3:4-10, ... *"For while one saith, I am of Paul; and another, I [am]of Apollos; are ye not carnal?*

5 who then is Paul, and who [is] Apollos, but ministers by whom ye believed, even as the Lord gave to every man?

6 I have planted, Apollos watered; but God gave the increase.

7 so then neither is he that planteth any thing, neither he that watereth; but God that giveth the increase.

⁸ now he that planteth and he that watereth are one: and every man shall receive his own reward according to his own labour.

⁹ For we are labourers together with God: ye are God's husbandry, [ye are] God's building.

¹⁰ According to the grace of God which is given unto me, as a wise master builder, I have laid the foundation, and another buildeth thereon. But let every man take heed how he buildeth thereupon"

This is a total demonstration of the divine wisdom of God.

The Wisdom Of Nations

The Bible says *"the fear of God is the beginning of wisdom."* I would like us to examine four nations of the world and the kinds of wisdom that influence them: the two Koreas, that is North Korea and South Korea.

North Korea

Kim Jon Ill succeeded his father as the president of the North Korean Republic, just a boarder away from the south. The North has refused our Almighty God as the creator of the universe and is seriously

THE RELEASE OF DIVINE WISDOM

against planting of churches, against freedom of its people and against private establishment. This same communist country is one of the world's poorest in the Eastern world. It's still being fed by United Nations and its sister South Korea, who they are against bitterly. Satan has stolen their hearts and minds to their destruction.

Ironically the state of North Korea has numerous natural resources that could produce food and create wealth for her citizens. The only thing they could produce for now with their minds and hands are weapons of mass **destruction.** How true the statement is that the fear of the Lord is the beginning of wisdom! And God is the ruler among the nations of the earth.

See the result of human, earthly and sensual wisdom at its best: hunger, poverty, cruel invention and lack.

Suddenly, North Korea has become a thorn in the flesh among the nations of the world, with Iran also following suit; how sad. However God is still on the throne ruling in the affairs of men.

There are, I must indicate, genuine born-again believers who are operating underground, praying and speaking in tongues for God to change things in the country of North Korea. No wonder Satan loves to operate when the children of God gather at His feet.

Job 1:6-9, "*Now there was a day when the sons of God came to present themselves before the LORD, and Satan came also among them.*

And the LORD said unto Satan, Whence comest thou? Then Satan answered the LORD, and said, from going to and fro in the earth, and from walking up and down in it.

And the LORD said unto Satan, Hast thou considered my servant Job, that [there is] none like him in the earth, a perfect and an upright man, one that feareth God, and eschewed evil?

Then Satan answered the LORD, and said, doth Job fear God for nought..."

South Korea

The Eastern nation is the place where we can find some of the world's largest churches globally:

    The largest Charismatic church.
    The largest Presbyterian church.
    The largest Baptist church.

Here, most of the leaders of the nation are serious born-again believers spirit-filled, tongues-talking folks, through the influence and power of speaking in tongues, prayer has transformed the entire nation.

THE RELEASE OF DIVINE WISDOM

Dr. David Yonggi Cho pastors the largest church in Korea. He says most of the military leaders and the prime minister serve as ushers in their ministry at the Yoido Full Gospel Church. South Korea is one of the economic tigers in Asia. Their secret, I believe, comes from the Bible. Why? Every true transformation comes from enlightenment; this liberates the human mind and finally triggers creative brains into productivity hence wealth.

SOUTH KOREA - THE LESSON

If entire nations would surrender to God through prayer, fasting and in humility, their blessings would be tremendous. He said, **"South Korea has greatly been inspired by God to the point they can now produce things on their own."**

North Korea is yet to manufacture its own car and airplane, but it is one of the leading producers of ammunition, weapons, rocket, nuclear warheads and missiles, etc.

However, South Korea, apart from U.S.A. and Japan, their cousins, is the third largest car manufacturing country on earth. The likes of KIA Motors, Hyundai Motors and electronics giants like Samsung and LG, just to mention a few, are from that country.

Speaking in tongues will open the heavens up for witty inventions and spiritual transformation. South Korea is the second largest country that sponsors and sends missionaries around the globe. May the Lord bless the works of their hands.

Psalm 90:16-17, *"Let thy work appear unto thy servants, and thy glory unto their children. And lit the beauty of the Lord our God be upon us: and establish thou the work of our hands upon us; yea, the work of our hands establish thou it."*

Speaking in tongues was reconnected by Dr. David Younger Cho. Therefore, do not be left out, start to speak in tongues right now for your spiritual transformation. When there is transformation in the spirit realm, it eventually affects and influences the natural. During the reign of Solomon, the land of Israel saw plenty and abundance; wisdom is synonymous with wealth and creativity. In other words, the wisdom you possess should bring you money and comfort!

The Wisdom Of Dr. David Oyedepo

One of the most used and accomplished generals of God in our time said: **"I would take my ministry team into the mountain top when we fasted and prayed in tongues for hours upon hours."**

THE RELEASE OF DIVINE WISDOM

Praying in tongues makes miracles happen. When you pray in tongues for hours, it clears your physical mind for divinely inspired thought, ideas, vision, and motivation to possess your spirit man. There couldn't be any wisdom than this. This same man, through the wisdom from speaking in tongues, has built a world-class university without borrowing from the bank.

Built 50,000 seater church within a year without borrowing from the bank. Currently he is building yet another university. Without wisdom you cannot build. He has also purchased three hundred brand new buses without borrowing from the bank. Where on earth did he get the money? Bible says a house is built by wisdom and not money. To unlock your divine destiny, you must pray more in **tongues.** That is the secret that brings the **wisdom.**

Every major ministry or every successful man I have ever encountered has in one way or the other attributed its/his success to covenants, obedience and prayer. They have said that the secret (mystery), the hidden element of their success, has always been speaking in tongues in their prayer closet for hours of prevailing prayer. You can't prevail with God in the flesh except for by the spirit when we pray.

"Likewise the spirit also helps our weakness: for we know not what we should pray for as we ought but the spirit himself makes intercession

*for us with groanings which cannot be uttered. And he that searches the hearts knows what is the mind of the spirit, because he makes intercession for the saints according to the will of God..." (**Rom. 8:26-27**).*

Our understanding is unfruitful; howbeit; the Holy Ghost, who baptizes us with the ability to speak in tongues, takes our prayers to God, where He does intense intercessions for only those who speak in tongues.

That is not to say God does not answer the prayer of folks who do not speak in tongues, but the ultimate plan of God is for us to pray or effectively communicate with Him through prayer, and prayer – speaking in tongues.

Great servants of God like King David, Prophet Isaiah and the rest wished they could speak in tongues. This was reserved by God for our generation. Praise GOD how blessed we are to speak in tongues.

The Generation of Tongues Speakers

I am a prophet by the grace of God and not by my doing or any special thing. I have been born again for almost twelve years now. I had such a strong passion to study God's word, pray and prophesy.

However, I realized I could not pray for a longer time, I either fell asleep or left the prayer to watch television. But one day something happened: I had an encounter, after which I could pray for four to seven hours nonstop. That was when my real spiritual transformation and maturity began. Immediately, people could see it and began to call me names like pastor, evangelist, just name it.

My secret comes from the encounter I had with tongues speaking. Peter's generation spoke in tongues; Paul's generation spoke in tongues. You can speak in tongues for divine wisdom! Jesus demonstrated wisdom in Matt 13:54b

"...whence halt this man this wisdom and this mighty works..."

The pagans couldn't stand the wisdom of Jesus at all. What we must understand is that wisdom is not synonymous with age, tribe, family or education. Paul equally boasted of his wisdom in the revelation of Jesus Christ.

"Wherein he hath abounded toward us in all wisdom and prudence" **(Eph 1: 8)**

Read 1 Cor. 2-3 for wisdom Scriptures.

8

The Release Of Glory

If there is one word that thrills a Christian's heart, its the word *glory*. The Longman Contemporary English Dictionary defines the word *glory* as "something that is especially beautiful, or makes you feel proud."

The reason for murder, rape, suicide and the destructive pain people inflict on themselves is the absence of the supernatural glory in their lives; they see life as a war and lacking meaning… therefore they find no reason to live life to the fullest, hence their early exit from the surface of the earth to hell. Light attracts, King Herod and the wise men saw the star **"glory"** of Jesus, though all were attracted. King Herod had an evil intention about the glory of Jesus. He made a speech and did not give God the glory, and was killed by the angels of God. You see, the pagan King Herod even wanted God's glory; how much more you and I who believe in the almighty

God, the giver of glory,

Matt. 2:7-12
⁷ "Then Herod, when he had privily called the wise men, enquired of them diligently what time the star appeared.

⁸ And he sent them to Bethlehem, and said, Go and search diligently for the young child; and when ye have found [him], bring me word again, that I may come and worship him also.

⁹ When they had heard the king, they departed; and, lo, the star, which they saw in the east, went before them, till it came and stood over where the young child was.

¹⁰ When they saw the star, they rejoiced with exceeding great joy.

¹¹ And when they were come into the house, they saw the young child with Mary his mother, and fell down, and worshipped him: and when they had opened their treasures, they presented unto him gifts; gold, and frankincense, and myrrh.

¹² and being warned of God in a dream that they should not return to Herod, they departed into their own country another way."

Papa God is an embodiment of glory. It's His glory in us that makes us the light of the world as

THE RELEASE OF GLORY

Christians. Glory is our divine nature; anything short of it is fake. When a child of God is at peace with God, there is such an unspeakable joy which wells up within his/her spirit. Its sweet, it's awesome, it's powerful!

After the earthly ministry of Jesus Christ, He humbly asked God to glorify Him and the works he had done. Many have the notion that God does not share his glory with anyone; you see, my friend, that is an Old Testament mentality.

> ***John 17:5-7*** *"...and now, O Father, glorify thou me with thine own self with the glory which I had with thee before the world was.*
>
> *⁶ I have manifested thy name unto the men which thou gavest me out of the world: thine they were, and thou gavest them me; and they have kept thy word.*
>
> *⁷ now they have known that all things whatsoever thou hast given me is of thee..."*

We believers represent the glory of God on earth. Without that, it means God can't manifest Himself on earth, so we are partakers of his divine nature (Ezekiel 28:22b).

> ***2 Pet. 1:3-4****, "According as his divine power hath given unto us all things that [pertain] unto life and godliness, through the knowledge of him that hath called us to glory and virtue:*

⁴ Whereby are given unto us exceeding great and precious promises: that by these ye might be partakers of the divine nature, having escaped the corruption that is in the world through lust..."

The word **glory** means **to shine, to bright, to illuminate, and to light up.** The Bible says God is light and in Him is no darkness at all. To have this light is to have God, which makes you the light of the world. So you can't be a light and not shine. Your ability to shine is directly proportional to your relationship with God!

In the book of Isaiah, God warned the Israelites not to use his name in vain, because some worshiped idols and other objects by depicting these things as **'God'.** This bitterly angered God, for he had said:

"...my Glory will I not share with any man either with graven image..."

Man made images to worship as 'God', forgetting the true God of Israel who created the heavens and the earth. Do you remember Aaron and Moses in the wilderness? Once Moses went to the mountain top to meet God, the children of Israel quickly gathered to themselves pieces of gold, melted them together as a golden calf and began to worship it.

The reason why people do not believe in God is simple: they can't see God. Therefore, in their minds

He doesn't exist. The same reason made the children of Israel in the wilderness worship idols as they pressured Aaron to sin. But the Bible admonishes us to believe although we have not seen.

> **John 20:29,** *"...Jesus saith ...... blessed [are] they that have not seen, and [yet] have believed..."*
>
> *(AMP) "... Blessed and happy and to be envied are those who have never seen me and yet have believed and adhered to and trusted and relied on me..."*

This has brought about the whole subject of faith and faith teachings. Apostle Thomas was nearly a victim to seeing is believing. However, in the New Testament Jesus prayed a prayer asking God to glorify Him. The question is: if we can't share in God's glory, why are we called men of God.

Why did Jesus ask the father to glorify him (John 17:22). In fact, please take a deep reflection on this Scripture. He said *"the glory which you have given me, I have given them"* Now which people received this glory of God from Jesus? It's simple, the believers who believe in God almighty through Jesus.

Do not be afraid to say you represent this glory of God in your generation. It's not pride. The Bible says in Matt 5:16.

> *"...Let your light so shine before men that they may see your good works and give glory to your father in heaven..."*

Why will people give glory to your father in heaven? Because you reflect his glory! **Therefore we are the glory of God on earth.**

There is a crucial lesson to be leant here; for people to give glory to our father in heaven, it means our light must shine. In other words, you can't separate our life from the glory of God. This is a true affirmation that we are partakers of his divine nature, although in the earthly realm.

When you do the right thing as a child of God and attract persecution, name calling and sarcastic remarks, don't worry; it is because you are unique and carry the glory of God. Even satan wanted the glory of God by asking the angels to worship him. Children of God walk freely in His glory because He is our father.

In this regard, the speaking of tongues plays an important role in activating the release of God's glory in our lives and that of other believers. Once one catches the fire of this revelation, he/she will pass it on to others with ease and in simplicity. God only receives glory when we choose to glorify him with our life on earth.

So my precious and dear friend, you are the glory of God.

Thank God for the teaching of Rev. Chris Oyakhilome of Christ Embassy, who has challenged us not to relent in our effort in bringing glory to God our maker.

Jesus talked much about glory and it was released upon him as he brought his earthly ministry to a close (John 7:39). When you understand that God is not only for him but you as well, then you can desire more and more to walk in this glory. All the generations past had an unquenchable desire to walk in God's glory all the time.

Exod. 33:18, "and he said, I beseech thee, shew me thy glory."

Moses walked in the glory of God. We see him in the book of Exodus pleading of God to show him His glory as stated earlier. I know every genuine and sincere believer would look to see the glory of God. When God finally answered Moses' prayer, the guy went blind for a season, having seen the back of God.

Exo. 33:22, "....and it shall come to pass, while my glory passeth by, that I will put thee in a clift of the rock, and will cover thee with my hand while I pass by."

It's a pity some of us haven't even seen angels, talk less of face-to-face encounter with Jesus or God himself.

Do not be worried, Jesus said:

> *"...He that hath my commandments, and keepeth them, he it is that loveth me: and he that loveth me shall be loved of my Father, and I will love him, and will manifest myself to him..."* ***(John 14:21)***.

Did Jesus Speak In Tongues?

Please get into the car as we journey to the mount of transfiguration. I strongly believe one's speaking in tongues is the heavenly language between God, angels and the born-again believers. The mount of transfiguration demonstrates the power of tongues speaking; no wonder the heavenly hosts heard him and dispatched Moses and Elijah.

I believe that when Jesus spoke in tongues and the Heavens opened, Peter, James and John were amazed at how Jesus had transfigured.

The word transfigured means to change into something else.

> ***Mark 9:2-9***, *"... and after six days Jesus taketh [with him] Peter, and James, and John, and leaded them up into a high mountain apart by themselves: and he was transfigured before them."*

THE RELEASE OF GLORY

³ And his raiment became shining, exceeding white as snow; so as no fuller on earth can white them.

⁴ And there appeared unto them Elias with Moses: and they were talking with Jesus.

⁹:⁵ And Peter answered and said to Jesus, Master, it is good for us to be here: and let us make three tabernacles; one for thee, and one for Moses, and one for Elias.

⁶ For he wist not what to say; for they were sore afraid.

⁷ And there was a cloud that overshadowed them: and a voice came out of the cloud, saying, this is my beloved Son: hear him.

⁸ And suddenly, when they had looked round about, they saw no man any more, save Jesus only with themselves.

⁹ And as they came down from the mountain, he charged them that they should tell no man what things they had seen, till the Son of man were risen from the dead."

What language was Jesus communicating in with Moses and Elijah? These saints had come directly from heaven. I believe they spoke in tongues, because Peter and the rest of the disciple were afraid they didn't understand the language. You only get afraid of things you can't comprehend.

Two Lessons

- Jesus received divine instructions and directives as Moses and Elijah ministered to him.
- God altered His natural countenance into the glory and nature of God. When you see the manifested glory of God, you will never be the same again.

Let's observe the reaction of Peter, **Mark 9:5**.

"...and peter answered and said to Jesus master it is good for us to be here..."

To be where? Note He said **HERE**. 'Here' means where the glory of God is. Peter has seen the wind blowing things and the supernatural moves of God's power and presence and therefore wouldn't dare move to any other avenue, any other place.

"...and let us make three tabernacles, One for you, one for Moses and one for Elias ..."

Probably for me too because I strongly desire to see more of God's glory in my life, miracle ministry and my relationships with others. So help me God. No man has seen the glory of God being the same.

My dear reader, I write in the middle of the night **today, Wednesday 1:37am (local time)**. Permit me to talk more on the glory of God. Let's fly back into the book of Acts of the Apostle, chapter four.

Experience Of God's Glory

Do you now see the connection between (Mark 9:2) the transfiguration experience and that of Acts 2:1 when the disciples received the Holy Ghost baptism and divine enablement to carry out the master's plan and will for their lives.

Jesus was not encouraged by any, but by two great servants of God, Moses and Elijah. Moses came thousands of years before Elijah but God choose them to appear at the same time to honor Jesus on the mount of transfiguration.

The Bible says *"suddenly there came a voice from heaven endorsing Jesus Christ the true son of God."* In the book of Acts, a similar scene transpired. Let's recount another *"suddenly"* in Acts 2:1. This time round it was the Holy Ghost himself who had to empower the believers to do the work of the ministry.

> ***Acts 2:1-4****, "AND WHEN the day of Pentecost had fully come, they were all assembled together in one place,*
>
> *² when suddenly there came a sound from heaven like the rushing of a violent tempest blast, and it filled the whole house in which they were sitting.*
>
> *³ And there appeared to them tongues resembling fire, which were separated and*

distributed and which settled on each one of them.

⁴ and they were all filled (diffused throughout their souls) with the Holy Spirit and began to speak in other (different, foreign) languages (tongues), as the Spirit [1] kept giving them clear and loud expression [in each tongues in appropriate words]."

The verse 4 says *"they were all filled with Holy Ghost and began to speak in tongues as the spirit gave them utterance..."*

Why on earth will the Holy Ghost cause the people to speak in tongues? The more they spoke in tongues, the more the increase of God's glory on them. Here we can say the glory of God was released through the act of speaking in tongues?

Speaking in tongues can actually change our lives and ministry forever. Same way the experience of the apostle's power and glory. The Bible says they were amazed; nothing beat the imagination and understandings of human kind. **Most definitely spectacular and supernatural.**

Apostle Paul said *"I thank my God I speak in tongues more than ye all.* **1 Cor. 14:18.** You know what? There is something unique about speaking in tongues.

The prophet once had a glimpse into the latter glory and cried to the Lord and said oh God let your glory fill the earth.

Isa. 6:3*, "And one cried unto another, and said, Holy, holy, holy, [is] the LORD of hosts: the whole earth [is] full of his glory."*

Paul commanded us to boast in the Lord. We carry the glory of God and that is true and nothing can take us from the glory of God. When God's glory is experienced or revealed to your spirit man, virtually nothing can stop you from dying for God. This passion was the reason Paul wrote Romans 8:30-38, *"…what can separate us from the love of God…'*

Zion Remembered

Psalms 137:1-4*, "By the rivers of Babylon, there we sat down, yea, we wept, when we remembered Zion.*

² we hanged our harps upon the willows in the midst thereof.

³ for there they that carried us away captive required of us a song; and they that wasted us [required of us] mirth, [saying], Sing us [one] of the songs of Zion.

⁴ how shall we sing the LORD'S song in a strange land?"

Captivity is not pleasant, neither is it comfortable. The folks here had tasted the glory of God in Israel and God's provision in the wilderness. **They could not but shout out** when Nebuchadnezzar ushered them into slavery and captivity for almost seventy years. One statement thrills my heart: *"... How can we sing the Lords song in a strange land...?"*

Obviously impossible. If you kind of find yourself in a strange land, start to speak in tongues; it will trigger an uncommon idea in your spirit and heart.

For you to maneuver your way through the storms of life, speaking in tongues will breakdown the chains of oppression from any task masters.

If you study the book of John, it talks about John's conviction about Jesus. He recounts, *"...we beheld his glory, as the only begotten of the father, full of grace and truth..."* **(John 1:14)**.

The Glory Released By Tongues

The glory released by tongues transformed the Apostle into a superman, like some of us today who in time passed had no hope but are now counted worthy of the Lord. By his grace we are now considered worthy of the Lord; we are called men of God, when in actual sense were the enemies of God.

When you speak in tongues, it will squeeze out the deposit of glory in you for manifestation, thereby

THE RELEASE OF GLORY

culminating in beauty and glory all the days of your life! The glory is released through divine encounter.

Several people have been given supernatural encounters from the Lord to register an imprint on their minds. Jesus was such a man; Apostle Paul was another, on the road to Damascus to persecute the Christian. (Acts 9).

> **Acts 9:1-9,** *"MEANWHILE SAUL,* [1] *still drawing his breath hard from threatening and murderous desire against the disciples of the Lord, went to the high priest*
>
> *² And requested of him letters to the synagogues at Damascus [authorizing him], so that if he found any men or women belonging to the Way [of life as determined by faith in Jesus Christ], he might bring them bound [with chains] to Jerusalem.*
>
> *³ Now as he traveled on, he came near to Damascus, and suddenly a light from heaven flashed around him,*
>
> *⁴ And he fell to the ground. Then he heard a voice saying to him, Saul, Saul, why are you persecuting me [harassing, troubling, and molesting Me]?*
>
> *⁵ And Saul said, who are You, Lord? And He said, I am Jesus, Whom you are persecuting.* [2]

UNDERSTANDING TONGUES SPEAKING

It is dangerous and it will turn out badly for you to keep kicking against the goad [to offer vain and perilous resistance]."

⁶ Trembling and astonished he asked, Lord, what do you desire me to do? The Lord said to him, but arise and go into the city, and you will be told what you must do.

⁷ The men who were accompanying him were unable to speak [for terror], hearing the voice but seeing no one.

⁸ Then Saul got up from the ground, but though his eyes were opened, he could see nothing; so they led him by the hand and brought him into Damascus.

⁹ And he was unable to see for three days, and he neither ate nor drank [anything]."

God released him into a dramatic encounter that changed him forever. Kenneth Hagin of blessed memory told his story of how God had him healed of tuberculosis miraculously on his bed of affliction. He said in his life and ministry, Jesus appeared to him more than eight times.

Such men and women who had encounters took their callings and ministries seriously. This is because they came directly in contact with the glory of God. No wonder his ministry is still in existence even after his death. Speaking in tongues ignites the power within and the power above for supernatural performance.

Glory At The Corridor

One man of God who has blessed me so much with divine truths and scriptural revelation is Pastor Chris of Christ Embassy. He narrated his story of how after a prolong fasting and prayer he began to sip fruit juice in his sitting room. All of sudden, a bright light of glory shone through to the corridors he got up to see the bright light, only to see it gently disappear. After seconds, this same glory reappeared, and before he could say Jack, Jesus surfaced from the light of glory right in front of him in his room. He recounts of how he immediately melted like a candle in a hot pan. He said it was as though there were no bones left in him.

If you see the glory of Jesus, your life will never be the same again. Guess what, Pastor Chris has a little book on tongues speaking and he is a strong advocate of speaking in tongues all the time. In fact, do not cheat yourself and distance yourself from the power that comes with tongues speaking.

Space and time would not permit me to write about the numerous servants of God who have had similar supernatural visitations like Benny Hinn, (USA), Prophet Kakra Baiden (Ghana), and Rick Joyner of Morning Star Ministries.

If you don't speak in tongues, the power, miracles, revelations and some strategic anointing will elude you!

The Final Conviction

Prayer is mostly misunderstood by many of us. When light comes, darkness will immediately disappear. Prayer is a two-way communication. The word "co" means two or more. This gives us the understanding that after we have prayed to God, we allow him to speak to us too, either through the Scriptures or through the Holy Spirit's ministration, whichever way would be a blessing not to us only but to all.

Prayer drops the fire of God into our system. This fire is sometimes termed as 'anointing' or 'the presence of God', and when this Spirit covers you, your inner man's transformation becomes rapid. This is because when we pray, unction comes on us that produces what we call a "magnetic aura". Therefore praying in tongues releases the aura in a greater dimension to light up your glory in God.

Satan's Fear

Every believer carries a certain amount of glory, but those who speak in tongues activate it the more.

Therefore they become more powerful; demons can see this glory on believers.

Satan was afraid to touch Job because he saw a hedge of fire around him. May you have this same hedge of fire around you in Jesus' name Amen! When the glory of God is released upon you, supernatural manifestations become the order of the day; you sense at all times.

The Glory Of God Triggers The Healing And Prophetic Anointing

When you sense the glory or an anointing in your meeting, stretch forth your faith to do the impossible, lay hands on the sick, cast out demons and recover the sight of the blind in Jesus' name. Jesus took advantage of the glory that appeared on him at a marriage ceremony by turning water into wine. Your decision to walk in the supernatural will ascribe more glory to God. (Matt. 9:8). Jesus had a tremendous church growth because he decided to do what he did.

Nobody Can Resist Your Glory

The devil saw the works of Jesus and began to persecute him from every angle. In the final analysis, my Lord was killed (Crucified) on the cross. What was meant to be a celebration for the pagans and the Roman soldiers resulted in the multiplication of an unusual glory. According to Matthew's account, even the dead in cemeteries rose up that day. Glory to God!

> **Matt. 27:50-53,**
> *⁵⁰ "And Jesus cried again with a loud voice and gave up His spirit.*
>
> *⁵¹ And at once the curtain of the [15] sanctuary of the temple was torn in two from top to bottom; the earth shook and the rocks were split. (10)*
>
> *⁵² The tombs were opened and many bodies of the saints who had fallen asleep [16] in death were raised [to life];*
>
> *⁵³ and coming out of the tombs after His resurrection, they went into the holy city and appeared to many people."*

Mrs. Pilate

Mrs. Pilate sounded a strong warning to the husband not to have anything to do with Jesus because, in her own words, she suffered many things in her dream *(Matt 27:19)*. After Pilate's verdict, he boldly declared that he was innocent of the man's blood should he be killed.

Matt. 27:24 *"So when Pilate saw that he was getting nowhere, but rather that a riot was about to break out, he took water and washed his hands in the presence of the crowd, saying, I am not guilty of nor responsible for this* [3] *righteous Man's blood; see to it yourselves.*

Let His Blood Come Upon Us

What a prophecy! Immediately Pilate washed his hands off before the people, they simultaneously carried out demanding the blood of Jesus to come upon them. In contrast of their demand, God, who is wiser than man shared the blood of Jesus on the cross so that all could come to salvation.

Satan then thought he had succeeded in killing Jesus but in the wisdom of God, the crucifixion was bringing salvation to all who believe.

1 Cor. 2:8 puts it in a better way;

"...None of the rulers of this age or world perceived and recognized and understood this, for if they had, they would never have crucified the Lord of glory..."

Simply, he could not take the glory of God away from Jesus; neither can he take it from you. Go, walk in the glory; it's where you belong.

9

The Release Of Mysteries

The secret things belong to God, but the things which are revealed to us are for our good. Any time I am given an invitation to preach anywhere in the world, even after enough prayer and study of the subject matter, usually there is this nervousness that gripes me until I start to preach.

Why The Nervous Feeling

I have heard several great and small ministers of the Gospel talk about this same experience time and again. The truth is nobody knows the mind of God at all times and what he will do in every meeting, hence our nervousness. My friend, it is not as simple to know the will and mind of God as it may look. That is the nature and character of the God we serve. He loves to hide things from us to search them out. When we find them, then it becomes a revelation and a rhema to us.

Anything From God Is Mystery

Anything from God is a mystery until we discover it in the earthly realm. Moses at one point wanted to see God, this mysterious God, and the result was quite devastating. However, that is not to say we cannot understand God and his leadings in our lives as believers. Come with me as we embark on this journey to discover the mystery about tongues speaking.

The Bible says in **Matt. 13:11**,

> *"...And He replied to them, to you it has been given to know the secrets and mysteries of the kingdom of heaven, but to them it has not been given..."*

I want us to seriously compare this scripture to that of *1 Cor. 14:2*,

> *"...For one who speaks in an [unknown] tongues speaks not to men but to God, for no one understands or catches his meaning, because in the [Holy] Spirit he utters secret truths and hidden things [not obvious to the understanding]..."*

The Bible says **when you speak in tongues you speak unto God.** *"...howbeit in the spirit he speaketh mysteries..."* So we can say mystery begets mystery. To release the plan, secrets or the will of God for your life, you must intensively engage yourself in tongues speaking. When you pray in tongues your spirit contacts God's Spirit, where there is a massive flow of his grace, secrets and power into your spirit man. I must confess that it would be a life-long thing because the secrets of God are revealed to us in bit and pieces.

The Purpose Of Mystery

- *To conceal a matter*
- *To be selective*
- *To show class*
- *To defeat the enemy*

To control man from going ahead of God. Man has the tendency to go ahead of his Maker if he becomes all-knowing. Just like parents would desire their kids to ask them for help so they would help them out of their weakness and challenges, so is God happy each time or day we call or turn to him to help us.

Paul the Apostle saw lots of revelations which could easily make him boast, but had a weakness in his body that made him constantly go to God in prayer. Then God showed up to tell Paul that his grace was sufficient for him and his strength was made perfect in his weakness.

2 Cor. 12:9, *"And he said unto me, My grace is sufficient for thee: for my strength is made perfect in weakness."*

Can I dare say there have been several challenges you have prayed about but God is equally saying leave it alone for my grace is sufficient for you? You know, that makes God our papa and the Creator of the universe.

For God to put you ahead in life or on your colleagues if you study carefully. Various ministries have their first core value of their callings. We are all basically called to preach salvation, but salvation in itself is a package. Some preach salvation and prosperity, or salvation and church growth others also some preach salvation and morality or salvation, casting out demons and deliverance. Again some also preach salvation, God's grace and dominion, while others preach salvation, prophetic revelation and prayer.

The list could actually go on without end. When one sticks to his major calling, he turns to excel in his ministry. How do they get the burden to run on a particular line of ministry? This is a mystery, but it's revealed to the hearts of men in prayer and subsequently comes as a burden.

This is the reason why you cannot judge anybody's calling because people have different revelations and burdens of God. The mystery is only revealed to you

THE RELEASE OF MYSTERIES

in prayer and in studying the word. For you to have more mysteries revealed to you from the heart of God, you must spend quality time praying in the spirit or praying in tongues.

Col. 4:17 *"... Take heed to the ministry which thou hast received in the Lord, that thou fulfil it."*

To maintain a strong and solid relationship with Go you must d pray in tongues. The reason for the coming of Jesus was to bring mankind back to God and to restore the fellowship that existed before; basically what is still on God's mind is love and fellowship daily. He wants to share his secrets and blessings with us. So the more we stay away from him, the bigger we lost.

2 Cor. 12:1-4

"... I will come to visions and revelations of the Lord.

2 I knew a man in Christ above fourteen years ago, (whether in the body, I cannot tell; or whether out of the body, I cannot tell: God knoweth;) such an one caught up to the third heaven.

3 And I knew such a man, (whether in the body, or out of the body, I cannot tell: God knoweth;)

⁴ How that he was caught up into paradise, and heard unspeakable words, which it is not lawful for a man to utter."

There are certain visions and revelations you will never see without going to the presence of God in prayer. The more you speak in tongues the faster you receive revelations and visions. The Bible says the secret of the Lord is with those who fear him; the more you fear God the more he loves you that is why he sacrified Jesus for you. And this same Paul said to the Corinthian church that he thanks his God that he spoke in **tongues more than every one of them.**

From today onwards I want you to understand that you are God's friend. Start to communicate with God, develop a serious relationship with God. In this era of human communication-in the likes of internet, mobile phones ringing everywhere, destructing our focus and attention from God-we have got to decide to have quality time with God, regardless of the destructions.

God's will is a mystery **Eph. 1:9:**

"...Making known to us the mystery (secret) of His will (of His plan, of His purpose). [And it is this:] In accordance with His good pleasure (His merciful intention) which He had previously purposed and set forth in Him..."

The Bible says we are created in the image of God and in His image created He us, male and female. Once our origin comes from God, everything done on earth as our assignments must conform to the plan, vision and desire of God. This is what we call the Will of God - Knowing his plans and aligning yourself to it.

The quest to follow God's Will all your life is not always comfortable. There are several potholes in the journey of faith, but with Jesus in control, his sheep will not go astray. The will of man is always against the will of God.

Luke 22:42-43, *"Saying, Father, if thou be willing, remove this cup from me:.... not my will, but thine, be done.*

And there appeared an angel unto him from heaven, strengthening him."

As a result, many believers don't ever discover the will of God for their lives. Some have discovered, but, the sacrifices, brokenness, and the price to pay alone have sent potential vessels of God parking out of their calling.

You see, in the University of God, no matter how brilliant you may be, there are no shortcuts. You would have to take every course till you finish it. Come let's speak in tongues. NOW!

Discovering The Mystery Of His Will

Mysteries are meant to be discovered. As long as you can ask your dad for explanation on an issue, the same principle is applied when it comes to dealing with God. When you speak and pray in tongues for long in your prayer room or your closest, every mystery from God will become a revelation to you with ease.

My dear friend, you can't and may never achieve much for God if you do not know what he designed you for. His mystery surrounding your life can only be decoded by the power of praying in tongues for long hours.

Do you observe I keep emphazing long **HOURS** in prayer? It may never equally be so with you, but for me, all are not equal in comprehending or discerning spiritual things. Simply, all are different in fearing, different in serving. That is why I recommend to you the need to speak in tongues. I know what this has done for me and for others: it will open up your spirit to know what God's will is for the now and the future.

Mum Delivered From Heart Attack

I have trained myself not to sleep early at night. Mostly I retire to bed around 2am almost every day because my strength lies in the night; therefore I always take advantage. One night as I was watching CNN at midnight, the spirit of God ministered to my heart to start praying in tongues. Note, I did not have any idea as to what to pray about. I started speaking in tongues profusely.

Then five minutes later, I could hear myself rebuking my mum's condition of heart attack here and there. After the prayer, the spirit ministered to me about my mother's heart attack, but I still didn't believe because I had no information regarding her heart condition. The next morning I phoned my elder brother, who confirmed that my mother had suffered a severe heart attack the previous night.

God's eye sees every secret place and He is all-knowing. Sometimes His instruction might look very foolish from the beginning but in the end it will be the timely life-saving instructions ever received.

The Word Is A Mystery

Do you know people have read the Bible from cover to cover and still don't understand what is written in there? You can find out from the Rastafarian at the beaches or ask Mr. Satan why, because he knows the word of God too.

In the book of Ephesians, Apostle Paul prayed a prayer for the Ephesians church so God would open their eyes of understanding to the revelations packed in the word of God.

> **Eph. 1:16-19**, *"...I do not cease to give thanks for you, making mention of you in my prayers.*
>
> *¹⁷ [For I always pray to] the God of our Lord Jesus Christ, the Father of glory, that He may grant you a spirit of wisdom and revelation [of insight into mysteries and secrets] in the [deep and intimate] knowledge of Him,*
>
> *¹⁸ By having the eyes of your heart flooded with light, so that you can know and understand the hope to which He has called you, and how rich is His glorious inheritance in the saints (His set-apart ones),*
>
> *¹⁹ And [so that you can know and understand] what is the immeasurable and unlimited and surpassing greatness of His power in and for us who believe, as demonstrated in the working of His mighty strength..."*

Eyes Of Understanding

The human body has eyes to direct it successfully in the affairs of life. The same is so with our spirit man; he has spiritual optical lens and eyes that must see clear to direct both the body and the spirit. The eyes of the spirit see better than the eye of the body.

The eyes of the spirit are also called the eyes of God. Paul prayed for the Ephesus church that their eyes of understanding might be *"enlightened"*, which means to receive more transformation.

Whenever you don't receive revelation from Scriptures, pray the Ephesus prayer (Eph. 1:17-19), and within a matter of a day you would be amazed with the kind of revelation that would be made available to your spirit.

> **Eph. 1:17-19,** *"That the God of our Lord Jesus Christ, the Father of glory, may give unto you the spirit of wisdom and revelation in the knowledge of him:*
>
> [18] *"The eyes of your understanding being enlightened; that ye may know what is the hope of his calling, and what the riches of the glory of his inheritance in the saints,*
>
> [19] *"And what [is] the exceeding greatness of his power to us-ward who believe, according to the working of his mighty power"*

Your Mind Will Be Quickened

God has chosen the medium of mystery to deliver vital information to his children. The Bible says the ways of God are past finding out. The information from God is not received with the human intellect;

it is perceived by the human spirit that dwells in Him. Tongues speaking sharpens the sensitivity of the human spirit.

How can we get instructions from God, since his ways are past finding? The Bible says if we seek Him, we will find Him. Isa. 55:6, Matt. 7:7, Psalms 105:4, Psalms 27:8.

> **Ps. 27:8**, *"...You have said, Seek My face [inquire for and require My presence as your vital need]. My heart says to You, Your face (Your presence), Lord, will I seek, inquire for, and require [of necessity and on the authority of Your Word]..."*
>
> **Matt. 7:7-8**, *"...Ask, and it shall be given you; seek, and ye shall find; knock, and it shall be opened unto you:*
>
> *[8] For every one that asketh receiveth; and he that seeketh findeth; and to him that knocketh it shall be opened..."*

Speak in tongues more and more. AMEN!

10

The Release Of Precision And Accuracy

This chapter will be focusing entirely on the development of the inner man.

In the prophetic realm of operation, there is no such thing as trial and error; every prophetic word given involves human life and destiny... you either speak for God or self. Many voices could speak simultaneously, therefore knowing the prophetic voice of God and delivering it lies in one's maturity. Precision and accuracy is an excellent spirit of God. Precision and accuracy is the ability to receive and deliver a strategic instruction or message from God in maturity and wisdom. This spirit must be operational in every believer regardless of your educational background. Again, this spirit is not gotten from any educational institution but from the college of the Holy Spirit.

Watch-Out Hints

1. To operate in this realm requires you to become a born-again Christian.

2. An ability to interpret dreams accurately.

3. If you preach the word with revelation and power.

4. If you are regularly led by the Holy Spirit.

5. If God speaks to you through the Scriptures, which is the Bible.

6. If you are gifted with prophetic revelations.

7. If you can interpret tongues accurately.

8. If you operate in the spirit of wisdom.

9. If you can discern familiar spirits.

The spirit of precision and accuracy is always released by God to believers to defeat satanic lies and conspiracies. This same spirit was functional in the past and still is in our time. The points stated above are some of the attributes of people who speak in tongues and are baptized with the Holy Ghost. Therefore if your spirit man is not strengthened by prayer and speaking of tongues, precision and accuracy will surely elude you.

Growing In Precision And Accuracy

To grow in precision and accuracy, the inner man should be practically developed, trained and enhanced to receive strategic instructions.
Some of these factors can influence the rapid development of the inner man.

Maturity

Maturity in God does not come with age but the time spent standing with God in tough times and having his experience rub off you.

Job 32:6, *"...And Elihu the son of Barachel the Buzite answered and said, I [am] young, and ye [are] very old; wherefore I was afraid, and durst not shew you mine opinion. (7) I said, Days should speak, and multitude of years should teach wisdom. (8) But [there is] a spirit in man: and the inspiration of the Almighty giveth them (9) Great men are not [always] wise: neither do the aged understand judgment..."*

Perception/inspiration

Training your spirit to catch signals that are from God.

Acts 27:10, *"...And said unto them, Sirs, I perceive that this voyage will be with hurt and much damage, not only of the lading and ship, but also of our lives..."*

Alone with God

Mark 1:35, *"... And in the morning, rising up a great while before day, he went out, and departed into a solitary place, and there prayed..."*

Sensitivity

A man of God, though in a crowd, could still be sensitive to the ministration of the spirit to his heart.

Daniel

In the whole of the Babylonian empire, men of understanding were sent for; magicians were also called on, to contact their mediums, yet none was better.

Precision and accuracy is the spirit from God which causes man to know events from the past, to the present and the future. No one can know these things except the fellow is born by the spirit of God in heaven who reveals all secrets from generation to generation.

As the name implies, this spirit is able to deliver the most hidden detail / secret / information from the hearts of men to the man of the spirit, so that when mentioned it beats the imagination and understanding of man.

Babylon

Dan. 2:19, 22: *"Then was the secret revealed unto Daniel in a night vision. Then Daniel blessed the God of heaven.*

²² He revealeth the deep and secret things: he knoweth what [is] in the darkness, and the light dwelleth with him

God is the brain and master architect behind this supersonic revelational ability.

Is prophecy different? You can't separate it from the spirit of precision and accuracy. When you mature in the prophetic ministry, you would realize prophecy is all about precision and accuracy. The fire power for this operation in the ministry is speaking in tongues. Tongues here give your spirit man sensitivity. It is the initial instrument for operating in precision and accuracy.

Here you have total control over the voice of your flesh. So when the spirit speaks, you can clearly distinguish between the spirit and the flesh. You get to the point where you are constantly led by the spirit of God. *(Romans 8:14)*, here, you can harness your relationship with the spirit of God.

> **Rom. 8:14,** *"...for as many as are led by the Spirit of God, they are the sons of God..."*

> **Acts 27:10,** *"...and said unto them, Sirs, I perceive that this voyage will be with hurt and much damage, not only of the lading and ship, but also of our lives..."*

Dreams

Dreams and visions become super abundant. God gives you the grace and ability to interpret dreams with such precision and accuracy. Many will call you a prophet of God because you have the secrets of God with you all the time.

Your words become oracles because of the spirit of accuracy and precision God gives to you. You simply know the mind of God. People will fill your residence; simply because they think you have solutions from God to their problems. This spirit demands order, humility and sobriety. Interpretation of dreams and visions become common.

Struggles become a thing of the past. Joseph operated in this realm. His outstanding grace and ability to interpret dreams brought him to a place of authority: from the prison to the palace. The same is the story of Daniel. This anointing brings people closer to God and God closer to the people. Paul also functioned in this anointing.

Authority

Must you be a pastor or a prophet to operate in this realm of the spirit of precision and accuracy? Any serious believer who remains faithful to God can function in this realm. This gift that comes with precision and accuracy will bring you recognition, but not among your own people. They will fight and criticize its origin, its authenticity and the vessel as well.

Note, when God used Daniel and Joseph greatly in these areas, they were careful in giving glory to God as their source, strength and provider of all things pertaining to hidden things.

Authenticity

When God recognizes your faithfulness, he might put you in a distressing position / situation where you will be uncomfortable. The discomfort will cause you to pray and fast more. When developed, nothing in this state can escape the microscope of your spirit, because He knows that if he reveals something evil, you will not sleep but would do something about it.

PLEASE NOTE

Spiritual events and activities are no more secrets to you. Thank God for the spirit of precision and accuracy.

ONE POINT...

Any time your spirit man becomes uncomfortable, it might mean something evil or a disaster is going on or is about to strike. To curb it means to start praying seriously in tongues. From the start, God might not show you what's on the way until you have prayed in the spirit. When you have finished with the prayer, God can choose to reveal it to you or not; the power and choice lie with Him.

www.ingramcontent.com/pod-product-compliance
Lightning Source LLC
Chambersburg PA
CBHW060810050426
42449CB00008B/1622